What's up with my
CAT?

What's up with my
CAT?

Dr. Bruce Fogle

DK Dorling Kindersley
LONDON, NEW YORK, MUNICH,
MELBOURNE, DELHI

First published in the United States 2002
by DK Publishing, Inc.
95 Madison Avenue, New York, NY 10016

2 4 6 8 10 9 7 5 3 1

Copyright © 2002

Dorling Kindersley Limited
Text copyright © 2002, Bruce Fogle
The right of Bruce Fogle to be identified as
Writer of this work has been asserted by him
in accordance with the Copyright, Designs,
and Patents Act 1988.

Library of Congress Cataloging-in-Publication
Data

Fogle, Bruce
  What's up with my cat? / Bruce Fogle.-- 1st
American ed.
    p. cm.
ISBN 0-7894-8405-6 (alk. paper)
  1. Cats --Diseases. 2. Cats--Health. I. Title.

SF985.F65 2002
636.8'0896--dc21
            2001047626

What's Up With My Cat? provides general
information on a wide range of animal health
and veterinary topics. The book is not a
substitute for advice from a qualified veterinary
practitioner. You are advised always to consult
your veterinarian or other appropriate expert if
you have specific questions in relation to your
pet's health. The naming of any organization
or product in this book does not imply
endorsement by the publisher and the omission
of any such names does not indicate
disapproval. The publisher and author are
not responsible for any loss, injury, or damage
allegedly arising from any information or
suggestion in this book.

Color reproduced by Bright Arts, Singapore.
Printed and bound in Slovakia by TBB.

See our complete product line at
www.dk.com

CONTENTS

Introduction   6

How to use this book   7

PART ONE
YOUR CAT'S HEALTH

A life indoors or outdoors?   10

The age and sex of your cat   12

Examining your cat   14

What to look for   16

Basic procedures   18

Hidden messages   20

Vaccinating your cat   22

Infectious diseases   24

Dealing with wounds   26

External parasites   28

Internal parasites   30

Recognizing shock   32

Artificial respiration   34

Heart massage   36

PART TWO
SYMPTOMS CHARTS

General behavior   **40**

Lethargy   **42**

Changes in sound   **44**

Injuries   **46**

Bleeding   **48**

Eye problems   **50**

Ear problems   **52**

Scratching the skin and hair loss   **54**

Swellings and lumps   **56**

Lameness and limping   **58**

Loss of balance and coordination   **60**

Seizures and convulsions   **62**

Sneezing and nasal disorders   **64**

Coughing, choking, and gagging   **66**

Bad breath   **68**

Breathing problems   **70**

Changes in appetite   **72**

Vomiting   **74**

Diarrhea   **76**

Bowel problems   **78**

Distended abdomen   **80**

Excessive drinking   **82**

Urinary problems   **84**

Genital discharges   **86**

Labor and birth   **88**

Glossary   **90**

Index   **94**

Acknowledgments   **96**

INTRODUCTION

Cats are great companions. They are blissfully content bossing us around, training us to meet their demands, coaching us in how to give them the care, attention, and affection they feel is their due. And we love them for it. It is a cat's independence that we find so appealing, but it can also make them frustratingly difficult patients.

Being solitary hunters, cats' social relationships are "selfish." "Independence" is imprinted in their genes. And, when a cat is unwell, its natural behavior is to withdraw and hide. The ill cat does not want its predators to know that it is debilitated. This is a great survival tactic, but can be a real nuisance for the cat owner, as it means that he or she may be unaware of a medical problem. The signals that a cat gives out when it is unwell are far more subtle, and occur later in an illness, than those of a dog.

This book will help you interpret the subtle signs given off by an ill cat. However, a book can never be a substitute for professional knowledge and experience, so use it with caution and always contact your vet if you are at all concerned about your cat's health.

Dr. Bruce Fogle

HOW TO USE THIS BOOK

WHAT'S UP WITH MY CAT? is a complete practical guide to looking after your pet's health. The first section provides a guide to understanding your cat's behavior, observing its vital signs, preventing disease, and performing first aid. The second section consists of comprehensive symptoms charts that enable you to look up any physical or behavioral changes that your cat may be displaying and, by following the yes/no flow charts, to identify whether there is health problem and how you should proceed to deal with it.

This heading tells you that you are in the *Symptoms Charts* section of the book.

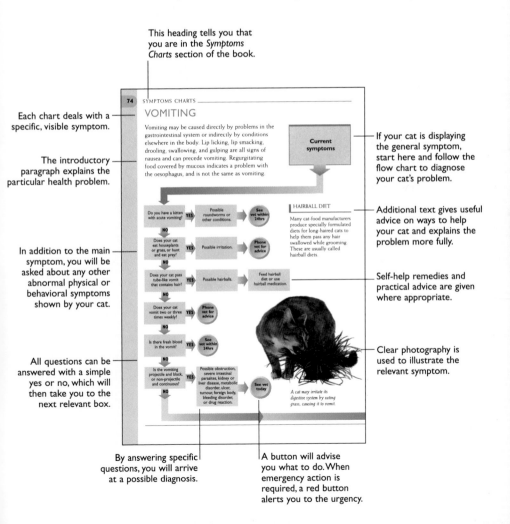

Each chart deals with a specific, visible symptom.

The introductory paragraph explains the particular health problem.

In addition to the main symptom, you will be asked about any other abnormal physical or behavioral symptoms shown by your cat.

All questions can be answered with a simple yes or no, which will then take you to the next relevant box.

74 SYMPTOMS CHARTS

VOMITING

Vomiting may be caused directly by problems in the gastrointestinal system or indirectly by conditions elsewhere in the body. Lip licking, lip smacking, drooling, swallowing, and gulping are all signs of nausea and can precede vomiting. Regurgitating food covered by mucous indicates a problem with the oesophagus, and is not the same as vomiting.

Current symptoms

If your cat is displaying the general symptom, start here and follow the flow chart to diagnose your cat's problem.

Do you have a kitten with acute vomiting! — YES — Possible roundworms or other conditions. — See vet within 24hrs

Does your cat eat houseplants or grass, or hunt and eat prey? — YES — Possible irritation. — Phone vet for advice

Does your cat pass tube-like vomit that contains hair! — YES — Possible hairballs. — Feed hairball diet or use hairball medication.

Does your cat vomit two or three times weekly? — YES — Phone vet for advice

Is there fresh blood in the vomit? — YES — See vet within 24hrs

Is the vomiting projectile and black, or non-projectile and continuous? — YES — Possible obstruction, severe intestinal parasites, kidney or liver disease, metabolic disorder, ulcer, tumour, foreign body, bleeding disorder, or drug reaction. — See vet today

HAIRBALL DIET

Many cat-food manufacturers produce specially formulated diets for long-haired cats to help them pass any hair swallowed while grooming. These are usually called hairball diets.

Additional text gives useful advice on ways to help your cat and explains the problem more fully.

Self-help remedies and practical advice are given where appropriate.

A cat may irritate its digestive system by eating grass, causing it to vomit.

Clear photography is used to illustrate the relevant symptom.

By answering specific questions, you will arrive at a possible diagnosis.

A button will advise you what to do. When emergency action is required, a red button alerts you to the urgency.

PART 1
YOUR CAT'S HEALTH

Lifestyle, sex, age, experience, and personality affect how a cat copes with injury or illness. To understand what's happening to your cat, it is important to know how to examine it, and what to look for. Learn to recognize not only its resting breathing and heart rates but also its gum color and blood pressure. Understanding how to use life-saving techniques prepares you to act efficiently when accidents occur.

A LIFE INDOORS OR OUTDOORS?

Your cat's lifestyle will affect its general well-being. While cats that are free to spend time outdoors lead more natural lives, they are also at greater risk of physical injuries and infections. The risk of tumors, for example, is higher. This is due to the relationship between certain viral diseases transmitted in other cats' saliva, and cancer of the lymph system, one of the most common forms of cancer in cats.

Most cats enjoy the freedom that comes with being allowed outdoors, but injuries and illnesses are more common in cats that venture outside.

INDOOR PROBLEMS

An indoor life is safer for cats, but for some individuals it can be seriously boring. While some cats are content with an indoor existence, inquisitive cats will create their own mental and physical activities to alleviate boredom. Some of these activities can be dangerous, such as hanging by the claws from window ledges, chewing on toxic house plants, and sleeping in the washing machine or clothes dryer. Observe your cat's behavior. Potential problems may be predicted, in part, depending on whether your cat is a hiding, reclusive introvert, or a dare-devil extrovert.

Indoor cats may be content, but watch for any signs of boredom that may lead to behavior that poses a risk to your cat's safety.

OUTDOOR CONDITIONS

Controlling what happens to your cat is more difficult if it is an indoor-outdoor cat that moves freely between the two environments. The great outdoors brings freedom and exhilaration, but it also brings a larger number of risks, including injuries from accidents, infections from animal bites, greater likelihood of allergies, and, unfortunately, higher risk of malicious injuries from air-rifle pellets, arrows, and poisons.

READING THE SIGNS OF ILLNESS

Pain is a perception. There are no specific pain pathways in the nervous system. Furthermore, the perception of pain varies between species. Cats, for example, are better at hiding their pain than dogs. This ability is both good and bad. On one hand, it means that cats do not develop pain-induced clinical shock (see page 32) as quickly as dogs. On the other hand, it means that a cat is less likely to reveal that they feel pain and, in the absence of complaint, we may not realize that our cat is seriously ill.

Whatever your cat's lifestyle, any change in its routine is important. The way it sits, the amount it eats, its relationship with you—all of these behaviors should be routine. If you detect any significant changes in your cat's routine, follow the suggestions provided later in this book on how to examine your cat. Always contact your vet for advice if you are concerned.

INHERITED CONDITIONS

Compared to many other species, cat breeding has not been subject to as much human interference. The fortunate result is fewer inherited breed-specific diseases. Conditions such as hereditary kidney, eye, and joint diseases do, however, occur. If you have a pedigree cat, find out about any health problems that are unique to the particular breed.

THE AGE AND SEX OF YOUR CAT

What happens to your cat is affected by its age and sex. All cats get up to mischief, but young cats are more likely to do things that a more experienced cat would not. Accidents, such as poisoning or trauma, are often high on the list of youthful misdemeanors. Female cats in season can behave very strangely, so be aware of what is normal before concluding that your cat has a medical problem.

Kittens are more likely to get into trouble than elderly cats, so keep all potential hazards out of reach.

BEHAVIORAL CHANGES WITH AGE

Cats are now living longer than ever before. In fact, geriatric medicine has now become a speciality in veterinary studies. As your cat gets older, it may slow down, become more aloof or more demanding, and its taste buds may change.

However, if you have a senior feline companion, do not assume that all changes in its behavior are just a consequence of growing older. Appetite and activity changes are also caused by illnesses such as an overactive thyroid gland or damaged kidneys. It can be difficult to differentiate between changes in your cat that are age-related and changes that are due to a medical problem. For example, eye changes may be caused by the inevitable accumulation of connective tissue in the lenses (sclerosis, an age-related problem) or by viruses (a medical problem).

Your elderly cat will benefit from twice-yearly veterinary check-ups.

If your older cat is not behaving normally, and, using the symptoms charts in the next section of this book, you cannot decide what is happening, always consult your vet. Elderly cats benefit from twice-yearly preventative check-ups. Visiting your vet before changes occur may prolong your cat's life.

YOUR CAT'S SEX

It is important to understand and differentiate sex-related activity from illness in your cat.

A female in season may surprise unwary owners. She may moan, wail, and drag herself around as if she has damaged her hindquarters—all activities that are easy to interpret as signs of pain and injury. She may drink more, become picky with her food, and change her toileting habits, urinating more frequently and in areas outside her litter tray. These are all normal sex hormone-related changes. Going off her food, drinking more, and depression may also indicate a life-threatening womb infection, however. If your cat is not neutered, become familiar with normal changes in behavior when she is hormonally active, so that you can better recognize when your cat is showing signs of being ill.

For intact male cats, the presence of a female cat in season can have dramatic consequences. It is not unusual for a male to go native when he scents a female in estrous. For example, a housetrained cat may start to spray pungent urine everywhere. If he goes outside, he is likely to fight with other males. He may even stop eating for a while.

NEUTERING A FEMALE

Females are induced ovulators. This means that they release eggs only after mating. If a female cat does not mate, another heat cycle will follow a few weeks later. This will continue until mating occurs. Neutered females live longer than unneutered females. Early neutering reduces or eliminates the risk of mammary tumors, the female's most common cancer. It also excludes the possibility of a womb infection or cancer of the reproductive organs, as well as the female cat's repetitive heat cycles.

NEUTERING A MALE

Neutering also prolongs a male cat's life expectancy, though for different reasons. It reduces the risk of rare prostate conditions later in life but, more importantly, it also reduces the frequency of fights with other male cats, minimizing the risk of lethal infections transmitted from cat to cat via contaminated saliva. From an aesthetic perspective, neutering will reduce a male cat's need to mark territory by spraying urine, as well as lessening the pungent aroma of the urine.

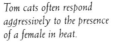

Tom cats often respond aggressively to the presence of a female in heat.

EXAMINING YOUR CAT

To find out what is happening to your cat, you have to examine it. In order to do this, you must have control over your cat. This is normally straightforward, but there may be occasions when your cat is frightened or in pain, and reluctant to be held or even touched. Restraint should be firm but gentle. Do not put yourself at risk of being clawed or bitten.

HANDLING YOUR CAT

From the time you first get your cat, train it to allow you to carry out a thorough examination. Practise examining your cat by including parts of an examination in routine play. During your practice examination training, do not try to do everything at once. This will be much too irritating for most cats. Instead, carry out partial examin-ations—for example, the head and neck, or the skin and coat. Allow your cat to become accustomed to being handled and carried by using food treats with strong odors, such as pieces of microwaved liver, prawns, and other delicacies that will tickle its taste buds.

Train your cat to associate a tasty food reward with a head-to-paw examination.

HOLDING A CALM CAT

Gently, but firmly, hold your cat's head under the chin. Apply light pressure against the cat's body with the elbow of your free hand while you carry out your examination with that hand.

Restrain your cat firmly by placing one hand under its chin.

HOLDING A FRIGHTENED CAT

Always use as little restraint as possible. Too much restraint upsets cats, making them even more uncooperative.

Talk reassuringly to your cat while calmly approaching. Do not stare directly at the cat as this is perceived as threatening.

Observe your cat's body language in an attempt to gauge its demeanor.

Do not risk being scratched or bitten by your cat. If you are uncertain how your cat will respond to your examination, use a large towel to pick it up.

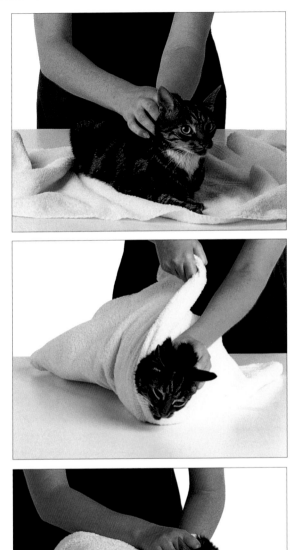

1 Place your cat on a bath towel, blanket, folded sheet, or any other available material. Hold the cat firmly by the scruff of its neck.

2 Wrap the material firmly around the cat, making sure that it cannot lash out with its teeth or claws.

3 Make sure that the cat's head is free while keeping the rest of its body safely cocooned. Hold the material around its neck to prevent it from unravelling. Carry out the examination only when your cat is calm.

WHAT TO LOOK FOR

VET'S ADVICE

MONITOR WEIGHT

It is sensible to monitor your cat's weight. To do so, accurate weighing scales are essential. A loss of 8 oz (225 g) might not sound like much, but to the average cat it is the equivalent of you or me losing 15 lb (7 kilos). An unexpected weight change is a sure sign that something is wrong with your cat.

See your vet within 24 hours if there is:

Weight loss and:
• Fever
• Lethargy
• Vomiting
• Diarrhea
• Lameness
• Changed appetite
• Altered drinking habits

Weight gain and:
• Lethargy
• Increased thirst
• Reduced appetite
• Dull coat
• Hair loss
• Shivering or shaking
• Vomiting

Understanding what is happening to your cat is partly passive, based simply on what you can see, smell, and hear. Knowing the cat's condition is also active, depending upon what you discover when you examine your cat. It is far easier to discover what is happening if your cat does not resent being examined.

Get to know your cat in order to understand its moods and behavior. As you examine your cat, note down your observations. Keep a record of the results and take this to your veterinarian when veterinary attention is required. Use the following chart as a guideline for your examination.

A HEAD-TO-PAW EXAMINATION

OBSERVE	RECORD
Observe your cat's behavior and responses.	Record any changes.
Listen to the sounds your cat makes.	Record any changes, and take action if necessary.
Watch your cat's activities and movements.	Record any changes, and take action if necessary.
Smell your cat all over.	Record any changes.
Monitor your cat's heart rate and breathing rate.	Record rates.
Check your cat's gums for color and capillary refill.	Record color and refill time.
Pinch the skin on the back of your cat's neck.	Monitor state of hydration.

A HEAD-TO-PAW EXAMINATION

OBSERVE	RECORD
Examine your cat's eyes, ears, nose, and mouth.	Record observations.
Examine your cat's head and neck.	Record observations.
Examine your cat's body and limbs, including its paws and nails.	Record observations.
Examine your cat's tail, anus, and vulva and mammary tissue or prepuce and penis.	Record observations.
Examine your cat's skin and coat.	Remove any foreign material and record changes.
Observe any gastrointestinal changes.	Record observations.
Monitor your cat's toilet habits.	Record changes.
Monitor your cat's eating and drinking activity.	Record changes.
Weigh your cat.	Record weight.

WORDLESS COMMUNICATION

It is only a surprise to people who have never lived with pets that words are not necessary for communication between a cat and its owner.

The way in which we understand our animals is very similar to the way in which we understand children before they have learned to speak. Through instinct and then learning, we understand how an infant feels or what he or she needs.

In a sense, cats are infants for life. With time, their ability to communicate how they feel improves, as our ability to understand what they are telling us increases. With experience, it becomes easier to understand your cat's wordless communication.

Record any changes in your cat's drinking habits. Excessive drinking may be an indication of illness.

BASIC PROCEDURES

An unwell or injured cat may need to be given medicine that has been prescribed by your vet. Getting your cat to take its medicine requires a gentle but purposeful approach. It is best to put the cat on a table or other raised surface and ask someone to help, if possible. You can wrap a difficult or frightened cat in a towel as shown on page 15. Do not try to hide a tablet in food since your cat may detect it and refuse to eat.

GIVING MEDICINE IN TABLET FORM

A cat needs to be held very still when it is being given a tablet, or other medicine, so if possible, ask someone to help you restrain it. Do not hold the cat too tightly and always talk to it in a reassuring tone of voice while you are giving the medicine.

CAT SCRATCH DISEASE

This rare infection, caused by a bacteria called *Bartonella henselae*, is transmissible to humans through cat bites and scratches.

While it rarely causes clinical illness in cats, it may cause a fever and tender, swollen lymph nodes in susceptible people, especially children and immune-suppressed individuals.

Cat scratch disease responds to antibiotic treatment. Fleas are the probable mode of transmission from cat to cat, possibly to people too, which is another reason to use an effective flea prevention.

1 While a helper holds the cat, gently enclose its head from above with your fingers. Do not ruffle its whiskers.

2 Grasp the head between forefinger and thumb and tip it back. Press lightly on the jaw to open the cat's mouth.

3 Place the tablet as far back as possible on the back of the cat's tongue.

4 Close the cat's mouth and gently stroke the throat to encourage it to swallow the tablet.

Hold the cat's head from above, while your helper holds its body firmly but gently.

GIVING LIQUID MEDICINE

An effective method for administering liquid medicine is by plastic syringe. Holding the cat's head at one side, squirt the measured, prescribed dose into its mouth. Give the medicine as slowly as possible so that it does not go down the wrong way.

Hold the cat's head while inserting the syringe between the teeth.

GIVING EAR DROPS

If your vet has prescribed drops for an ear ailment, administer them as quickly and carefully as you can, according to the instructions.

1 Using a piece of dampened cotton pad, wipe away any dirt from the inside of the ear.

2 Holding the cat's head firmly, fold the outer ear back and administer the required number of drops in both ears.

3 Be careful not to poke the dropper into the cat's ears. After administering the drops, gently massage the cat's ears.

Massage the drops gently into the ears for a few moments.

GIVING EYE DROPS

Eye problems diagnosed by your vet may require a course of drops to be given at home. Always continue treatment for as long as directed.

1 Gently clean the area around the eyes, wiping away any discharge from the corners with a small piece of dampened cotton pad.

2 Holding the cat's head firmly with one hand, apply the required number of eye drops in both eyes.

3 Allow the cat's eyes to bathe in the eye drops for a few seconds. Gently hold the eyes closed.

Hold the head up and gently keep the eye open.

HIDDEN MESSAGES

There are important external indicators that give valuable clues to the current state of your cat's health, but which are often overlooked. These are: the color of your cat's gums or the conjunctiva of its eyes; capillary refill time (the amount of time it takes for blood to return to your cat's gums after pressure has been applied); and the elasticity of the skin on your cat's neck. All these signs are vital clues to your cat's health. For example, a vomiting cat with normal gum color and capillary refill is not usually dangerously ill. In contrast, a vomiting cat with pale or white, red, or blue gums may be dangerously ill. Monitor these signs regularly so that you are aware when something is wrong with your cat. By regularly monitoring these signs, you are more likely to identify symptoms of illness as soon as they appear.

 VET'S ADVICE

CHECKING THE CONJUNCTIVA
If your cat is distressed when you touch its mouth, check its conjunctiva instead. Gently draw down the skin below your feline's eye to reveal the color of the conjunctiva. In healthy cats, it is pink.

CHECKING FOR DEHYDRATION

The elasticity of the skin on your cat's neck is usually a good indication of its state of hydration. In a healthy cat, when you pull up the skin on the top of its neck (a procedure known as "tenting"), the skin will snap back into its normal position immediately. To test for dehydration in elderly or fat animals, feel the gums. Dehydrated individuals have dry, sticky gums.

Why the skin may not snap back immediately

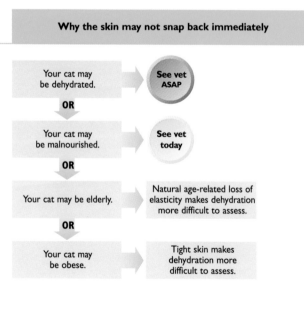

Your cat may be dehydrated.
OR
Your cat may be malnourished.
OR
Your cat may be elderly.
OR
Your cat may be obese.

See vet ASAP

See vet today

Natural age-related loss of elasticity makes dehydration more difficult to assess.

Tight skin makes dehydration more difficult to assess.

CHECKING GUM AND LIP COLOR

What color are your cat's gums or lips? What does it mean?

The color of your cat's gums indicates how much oxygen there is in its bloodstream. Lift a lip and look at the color of the gums or lips. Disregard any black pigmented areas.

Yellow	=	Your cat may have blood parasites, liver disease, or FIP (see page 25).	**See vet within 24 hrs**
Blue	=	Your cat may be in shock (due to oxygen deficiency).	**See vet ASAP**
White	=	Your cat may be in shock or it could have anemia or blood loss.	**See vet ASAP**
Pale	=	Your cat may be in early shock or it could have anemia or blood loss.	**See vet ASAP**
Pink	=	This is normal.	
Red	=	Possible bleeding in the mouth, carbon monoxide poisoning, fever, infection.	**See vet ASAP**

CHECKING CAPILLARY REFILL TIME

How long does your cat's gum remain blanched after applying pressure? What does it mean?

When blood is circulating normally, slight finger pressure on your cat's gums blanches the area under pressure. When pressure is relieved, the area instantly refills with blood.

Time		Meaning	
4 sec	=	Your cat is in deep shock.	**See vet ASAP**
2 sec	=	Your cat is in mild shock or has blood loss.	**See vet today**
1–2 sec	=	This is normal.	
Less than 1 sec	=	Your cat may have high blood pressure.	**See vet within 24 hrs**

VACCINATING YOUR CAT

Vaccination against infectious disease has been perhaps the greatest success story of 20th-century medicine. Diseases that commonly maimed or killed—polio in children, distemper in dogs, and enteritis in cats—have been virtually eradicated wherever preventative vaccination has become common policy. Routine vaccination eliminates the need for you to worry about a variety of infections that your cat may contract. Discuss with your vet the diseases your cat should be protected against and the frequency with which boosters need to be given. It is easy to forget how vital vaccinations are.

THE RISKS OF VACCINATION

Any veterinary procedure involves risk. The question you need to ask yourself is, "What is the risk from vaccination, and how does that compare to the risk of not being vaccinated?"

The scientific evidence
A report released in 2000 by the American Association of Feline Practitioners and the Academy of Feline Medicine Advisory Panel on Feline Vaccinations discourages the use of polyvalent vaccines (single injections that contain vaccine against many diseases), other than the vaccine that combines protection against flu and enteritis. The reporting bodies advise against combination vaccines because they "may force practitioners to administer vaccine antigens not needed by the patient," and because "as the number of antigens in a vaccine increases, so too does the probability of associated adverse events."

Vaccine-associated sarcomas
One of the "adverse events" the report alludes to is a skin tumor at the site of injection, a vaccine-associated sarcoma. These tumors occur more frequently in the US, where leukemia and rabies vaccines contain an "adjuvant" to enhance the potency of the vaccine.

A routine vaccination program can protect your cat against a variety of infectious diseases.

VACCINATION RECOMMENDATIONS

Feline Infectious Enteritis (FIE)
FIE is also known as feline panleucopenia and feline parvovirus. Vaccination is highly recommended for all cats. A booster should be given one year after primary inoculation, then as advised by your vet.

Cat flu
The term "cat flu" refers in particular to two viruses: rhinotracheitis virus and calicivirus. Vaccination against both viruses is highly recommended for all cats. A booster should be given one year after primary inoculation, as advised by your vet.

Vets should remind owners that inoculation only lessens the severity of illness–it does not offer full immunity. Moreover, there are several strains of calicivirus, and present vaccines do not provide protection against all of them.

Feline Leukemia Virus (FeLV)
Vaccination is recommended only for cats at risk, such as individuals that roam outdoors or live in cat shelters or households where new cats are frequently introduced. For these cats, annual vaccination is recommended. Vets recommend that cats with little or no risk of being exposed to the saliva of infected cats should not be vaccinated.

Your vet should remind you that vaccine does not induce protection in all cats. The best preventative is to avoid exposure to infected cats.

Feline chlamydia
This is an eye and upper respiratory infection. Routine vaccination is not recommended as the disease is not severe and can be treated effectively with an appropriate antibiotic.

Furthermore, research in North America has shown that the incidence of adverse side-effects is higher than with other vaccines although the vaccine has not been available for long enough in the UK to evaluate this.

Rabies
Rabies is caused by a virus that attacks nerve tissue. Infected animals tend to withdraw and avoid contact. Some become aggressive and may attack. Death always occurs once a rabies-infected animal shows signs of the disease.

Rabies is spread by bites or saliva of infected animals. If rabies is diagnosed, animals must be euthanized. Currently, 27 US states require rabies vaccination of cats. To protect your cat, and other cats or people who come in contact with your cat, you should vaccinate for rabies when your kitten is around 3 months or older.

OTHER FELINE DISEASES

Feline infectious peritonitis (FIP)
In the US, there exists an intranasal vaccine, but it cannot be given until a cat is 16 weeks of age. As most cats contract FIP around the time of birth, many experts question the value of this vaccination.

Feline immunodeficiency virus (FIV)
Research continues, but at present there is no vaccine against this disease.

 VET'S ADVICE

The vaccination advice given here is that of the American Advisory Panel on Feline Vaccinations. While these are generally sensible suggestions, following their advice is not always feasible. First, good catteries require up-to-date vaccination certificates. This usually means in accordance with the vaccine manufacturer's recommendations, which are nearly always for yearly rather than less frequent booster immunizations. Second, some pet health insurance policies insist on annual revaccination. Talk to your cattery and insurance company about any requirements.

INFECTIOUS DISEASES

Of all our pets, cats can harbor the most serious infectious diseases. Prevention and treatment of these conditions is often complicated and problematic. Many of these infections, almost all of which are viruses, are insidious. The disease may lie latent for years and years, or may apparently disappear, only to return when a cat is older, or when it is physically or emotionally stressed. A good understanding of how infections transmit themselves is vital if you are to prevent your cat from succumbing to diseases, especially those for which vaccines are not yet available.

A cat with a feline upper-respiratory virus, commonly known as "cat flu," may have a runny nose and eyes.

DISEASE	SYMPTOMS	TRANSMISSION
Feline Immunodeficiency Virus (FIV) FIV is not as aggressive as FeLV, and is not associated with tumors. With its long incubation period, FIV, like FeLV, is an eventual killer disease.	The signs of FIV are unpredictable but include: • Secondary infections from a variety of agents (this is because the immune system is suppressed) • Anemia associated with bone marrow suppression	As FIV is shed primarily in saliva, bites are the most common method of virus transmission. This is why male cats, who tend to fight more than females, are three times more likely to develop FIV infection than females.
Feline Infectious Enteritis (FIE)/Feline Panleucopenia/Feline Parvovirus This highly infectious yet preventable disease, known by several different names, can be fatal if left untreated.	• Severe vomiting and diarrhea, possibly with blood • Lethargy and listlessness • Dehydration	FIE is passed in the secretions and excretions of infected animals, or with contaminated materials. A cat with FIE remains infectious for weeks or even months. This is a very stable virus, and it can survive in a home, at room temperature, for a year.
Feline Leukemia Virus (FeLV) FeLV has a long incubation period, often years, and usually leads to serious, eventually fatal, disease.	The signs are unpredictable but include: • Development of white blood cell cancers such as lymphoma • Secondary infections from a variety of agents (this is because the immune system is suppressed) • Anemia associated with bone marrow suppression	The FeLV virus is shed by carrier cats in their saliva, urine, and other secretions. It is most commonly transmitted from a mother to her kittens around the time of birth. FeLV may also be passed through prolonged close contact with virus-shedding cats, their food and water bowls, and even their litter trays.

DISEASE

SYMPTOMS

TRANSMISSION

Upper Respiratory Tract (URT) Infections

A number of extremely contagious organisms may cause URT infection. Reovirus often only causes slight eye inflammation, while Chlamydia, a bacteria-like organism, causes significant inflammation that responds to antibiotic eye drops. Calicivirus (calici) and rhinotracheitis virus cause the most severe signs of URT infection.

A cat may recover from calici or rhinotracheitis infection–known as cat flu–but become a "silent carrier," appearing well, but infecting other cats. Rhinotracheitis is a "herpesvirus." This virus may reactivate under physical or emotional stress, causing renewed clinical infection.

Calicivirus and rhinotracheitis symptoms include:
• Sneezing, often with a thick nasal discharge
• Sticky or runny eyes
• Ulcers and open sores in the mouth
• Fever
• Loss of appetite associated with loss of smell
• Eye ulcers (caused by rhinotracheitis virus)
• Lameness and swollen joints in kittens (caused by calicivirus)

Herpesvirus is not spread in the air, but rather by direct contact, either with an infected cat or with its infectious secretions and excretions. The virus can remain infectious at room temperature for a month.

Calicivirus also spreads by direct contact with an infected cat, or items contaminated by its secretions and excretions. In some instances, it can be spread by an aerosol.

Chlamydia is spread from infected cats by secretions such as tears and saliva, while *Bordetella*, a cause of URT infection in dogs, can be passed from infected dogs to cats by aerosol transmission.

Feline Infectious Peritonitis (FIP)

Young kittens are most susceptible to this illness. The virus at first causes subclinical illness or mild diarrhea. It later changes its nature and becomes a killer.

The signs of FIP are unpredictable and divided into "wet" and "dry" forms.
Wet FIP may cause:
• Fluid build-up in the chest, causing difficulty in breathing
• Fluid build-up in the abdomen, causing the abdomen to swell and become distended
• Fever, vomiting, and diarrhea
• Weight loss

Dry FIP may cause almost any symptoms, including:
• Kidney failure
• Gastrointestinal disturbances
• Respiratory conditions
• Seizures
• Liver disease
• Lameness

There are two types of feline coronavirus: feline enteric coronavirus and FIP.

Both types of coronavirus are passed to kittens by mouth and nose contact with infected cat feces. At its worst, feline enteric coronavirus causes mild diarrhea in kittens, just after weaning. If a cat continues to suffer from the virus, the more serious and often fatal type, FIP, develops.

Rabies

This disease is invariably fatal and is also highly contagious to people.

The symptoms of rabies vary enormously, but include:
• Lameness
• Difficulty in swallowing
• Seizures
• Increased aggression or, rarely, docility

Rabies is transmitted in saliva, through a bite from an infected animal. Cats, however, are naturally somewhat resistant to infection. The virus is not stable and does not survive outside its host.

DEALING WITH WOUNDS

If you need to visit your vet with an ill or injured cat, make sure that the cat is comfortable during the journey, and that traveling does not make its condition any worse. Apply a temporary bandage to protect any wounds your cat may have, providing this does not stress the cat further. Be particularly vigilant with any closed wounds as these are potentially more serious than any visible injuries. If an emergency occurs, telephone your vet to explain what has happened, and to let him or her know that you are on your way to the veterinary hospital. This will give the veterinary team time to have everything ready for your arrival. Try to remain calm during your journey–panicking may result in dangerous driving, putting both you and your cat at risk.

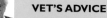

VET'S ADVICE

- **Do not pull large objects out of open wounds (for example, an arrow or a piece of wood), as this may cause uncontrollable bleeding. Instead, get help from your vet as soon as possible.**

- **Do not use petroleum jelly. It is difficult to remove later.**

- **Do not rub any wounds. Rubbing may result in further bleeding or damage.**

- **Do not underestimate small wounds. There may be considerable internal damage.**

SYMPTOMS OF A CLOSED WOUND

Closed wounds are less obvious than open wounds as the skin is not damaged. Your cat, however, may have considerable internal injury, and be in need of immediate veterinary assistance.

The symptoms of a closed wound include:

- Swelling
- Discoloration caused by bruising under the skin
- Pain
- Increased heat in a specific area

If you observe any of the above, your cat probably has a closed wound, and you should telephone your veterinarian immediately for advice.

DEALING WITH A CLOSED WOUND

1 If your cat has a closed wound, apply a cold compress as soon as possible. Lay a dish towel on the area (to prevent the cold compress from freezing the skin), then apply a bag of frozen peas. Keep in place for 15 minutes.

2 Your cat may have broken a bone. Splints are difficult to put on cats, but before taking your cat to the vet, make a lightweight splint with folded towelling. This will immobilize the injured area.

3 Carefully wrap the closed wound in several layers of material. Pin or tape the fabric–this will prevent it unravelling during the journey to the veterinary hospital.

If your cat has a wound, apply a bandage to protect the injury while you travel to the veterinary hospital.

SYMPTOMS OF
AN OPEN WOUND

Some open wounds are obvious, but others, such as those caused by fights, or air rifles may not be obvious as there is often little or no bleeding. All open wounds are exposed to dirt and bacteria, so the risk of infection is high.

The symptoms of an open wound include:

• Increased licking or attention to a specific area

• A new scab on the skin

• A skin puncture

• A trace of blood or simply moist hair on the skin

• Lameness

If you observe any of these symptoms, look for an open wound. If you find one, clean it, and then telephone your veterinarian for advice.

VET'S ADVICE

Watch for shock, especially if your cat has closed wounds that result from trauma. Shock is life-threatening. Treating shock, including the causes of shock, must take precedence over all else.

DEALING WITH
AN OPEN WOUND

1 If your cat has an open wound and it is not large, remove any obvious dirt, gravel, splinters, or other foreign objects with your fingers or a pair of tweezers.

2 Flush the wound with a little salt water, clean bottled or tap water, or 3 per cent hydrogen peroxide.

3 If the surrounding fur is getting into the wound, trim the hair. Before doing so, lubricate the scissors with a water-soluble jelly. This will ensure that the hair sticks to the scissors and not to the wound.

Use tweezers to remove any foreign bodies from a cat's paws (see step 1).

When dealing with an open wound, cut away the hair surrounding the wound (see step 3).

EXTERNAL PARASITES

Some parasites, such as ticks, fleas, lice, and ear mites, are visible on your cat's coat, while others, including other mites, yeast, and fungi, are hidden to the naked eye. Parasites may cause head scratching, a dull, dandruffy coat, inflamed skin without itchiness, itchiness with or without inflammation, or hair loss. As well as causing skin conditions, external parasites may transmit a variety of serious, even potentially life-threatening, illnesses. Advances in safe external parasite control mean there is no reason for any cat to suffer from skin parasites. Even so, parasitic skin conditions are still commonly diagnosed by vets.

Current symptoms

Are there any brown-gray, wart-like attachments on your cat? **YES** → Your cat has ticks. → Remove ticks immediately.

NO

Is your cat shaking its ears or scratching its head? Do its ears have a "sandy" deposit? **YES** → Your cat has ear mites (see page opposite). → Use an ear mite solution.

NO

Are there patches of circular hair loss anywhere on its body? **YES** → Your cat may have a fungal infection (ringworm) or flea dermatitis. → **See vet within 24hrs**

NO

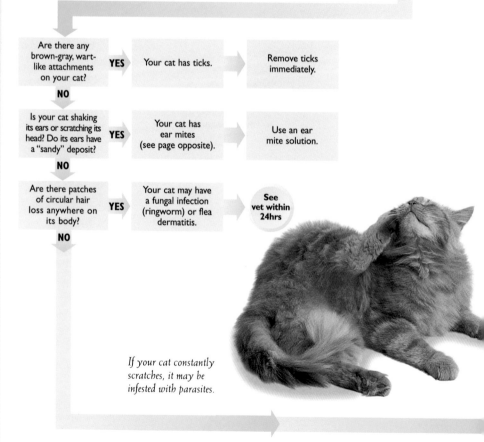

If your cat constantly scratches, it may be infested with parasites.

HOW TO DE-FLEA YOUR CAT AND YOUR HOME

Flea birth control
Use lufenuron, either a spot-on liquid or injection, on your cat. Any flea that feeds from your cat is effectively sterilized. Adult fleas then die of old age and your cat and home are cleansed of fleas.

This is a good product but it is not suitable for cats who are allergic to flea saliva. For these cats the fleas must be killed before they bite.

Flea killer
Use a spot-on liquid product such as imidocloprid, fipronyl, or selamectin.

Apply monthly as a drop on the skin of your cat's neck. Selamectin also kills scabies, ear mites, and roundworms. Fipronyl also kills ticks.

These products must be used with a household biological spray that prevents flea eggs from hatching.

HOW TO GET RID OF EAR MITES

Ear mites are very common in cats. Many kittens and most feral cats inherit ear mites from their mothers or from neighboring cats.

- Eradicating ear mites takes time. Those in the ears are easy to eliminate, with appropriate ear mite drops or a drop of selamectin on the skin of the neck. Dripping mineral oil into the cat's ears smothers most mites but does not get rid of any stragglers that may be lurking outside the ear canal.

- Ear mites are highly contagious. If one of your cats has ear mites, treat all your cats and dogs.

- Continue topical treatment for at least two weeks to ensure that you eliminate the problem.

HUMANS AND PARASITES

Some parasites affect humans:

- Fleas and ticks are equally at home on humans as on cats.

- Scabies mites can irritate and inflame human skin.

- Ringworm is highly contagious. It can be passed from cats to people, and vice versa. Immune-compromised people are especially at risk. Long-haired cats are more prone to ringworm but often have no clinical signs of infection.

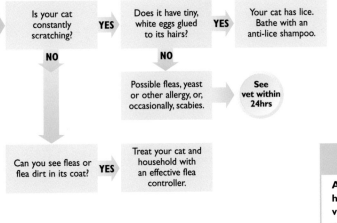

Is your cat constantly scratching? **YES** → Does it have tiny, white eggs glued to its hairs? **YES** → Your cat has lice. Bathe with an anti-lice shampoo.

NO ↓   **NO** ↓

Possible fleas, yeast or other allergy, or, occasionally, scabies. → **See vet within 24hrs**

Can you see fleas or flea dirt in its coat? **YES** → Treat your cat and household with an effective flea controller.

PRACTICAL TIP

After vacuuming your home, dispose of the vacuum bag as it may contain flea eggs.

INTERNAL PARASITES

Some intestinal parasites, especially the microscopic varieties, are not apparent until considerable damage has occurred. One of these parasites, *Toxoplasma*, can spread to humans via contaminated feces. Another– *giardia*–has become increasingly common worldwide. Intestinal parasites are preventable through the routine use of effective and safe medications.

Current symptoms

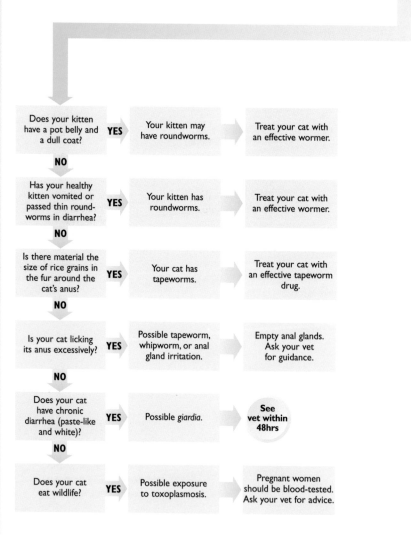

Does your kitten have a pot belly and a dull coat? **YES** → Your kitten may have roundworms. → Treat your cat with an effective wormer.

NO ↓

Has your healthy kitten vomited or passed thin round-worms in diarrhea? **YES** → Your kitten has roundworms. → Treat your cat with an effective wormer.

NO ↓

Is there material the size of rice grains in the fur around the cat's anus? **YES** → Your cat has tapeworms. → Treat your cat with an effective tapeworm drug.

NO ↓

Is your cat licking its anus excessively? **YES** → Possible tapeworm, whipworm, or anal gland irritation. → Empty anal glands. Ask your vet for guidance.

NO ↓

Does your cat have chronic diarrhea (paste-like and white)? **YES** → Possible *giardia*. → **See vet within 48hrs**

NO ↓

Does your cat eat wildlife? **YES** → Possible exposure to toxoplasmosis. → Pregnant women should be blood-tested. Ask your vet for advice.

MICROSCOPIC INTESTINAL WORMS

There are two important single-celled microscopic worms that may affect cats:

- *Giardia*, which causes diarrhea, can be contracted by people and cats. Like humans, cats acquire it by drinking contaminated water. Cats also contract it from eating infected wildlife, or from grooming paws that are contaminated by *giardia*.

- *Toxoplasma* is a single-celled parasite that seldom causes problems to an infected cat. However, toxoplasmosis can be transmitted to humans via contaminated cat feces (a cat passes infected feces only for a few weeks after its first exposure to the parasite). The disease is of special concern to pregnant women (a fetus infected with toxoplasmosis may develop serious problems) and to immune-compromised individuals.

Pregnant women should wear rubber gloves when cleaning a cat's litter tray, when gardening, and especially when handling raw meat. Eating undercooked meat should be avoided, as it is the most common way people contract toxoplasmosis.

Prevention and treatment
Use fenbendazole to treat a cat that has contracted *giardia*.
There is no simple treatment for toxoplasmosis. However, a cat that lives indoors cannot contract toxoplasmosis, unless it eats house rodents.

LARGE INTESTINAL WORMS

Roundworms are the size of small earthworms. Kittens often inherit them from their mothers, either via the placenta or in the first milk. They are the most common worms that kittens contract.
In an adult cat, the most common worm is the tapeworm, transmitted when a cat swallows a flea. If your cat has fleas, it is likely that it also has tapeworms.
Other worms, such as hookworms and whipworms, are rare in cats.

Prevention and treatment
Use a product such as imidocloprid, fipronil, or selamectin to control fleas, the intermediate host for tapeworms.
Veterinary licensed drugs are extraordinarily effective against the most common worms, especially praziquantel for tapeworms and roundworms, and fenbendazole for round-worms. These products can be used preventatively or therapeutically, according to your cat's lifestyle.

Use a recommended wormer to prevent your cat getting internal parasites.

HEARTWORM INFESTATION

Cats may also suffer from worms that affect the lungs and the heart. Heartworms are transmitted via mosquito bites. They occur in many regions of North America and continental Europe. If allowed to mature, worms clog part of the heart and major blood vessels around the heart, causing a gradual weight loss and a reduced capacity for exercise.

Prevention and treatment
Heartworm, which is more common in dogs than in cats, is preventable. Selamectin prevents heartworm, as well as fleas, ear mites, roundworm, and scabies. Several other once-a-month products prevent heartworm infestation.
If your cat goes outdoors, ask your vet about the local incidence of heartworm. Treatment involves a complex course of drugs.

RECOGNIZING SHOCK

The word shock has a specific medical meaning. Shock is the body's response to changes in blood flow inside the body. Changes in blood flow occur when there is internal or external blood loss, major injury, severe allergic reaction (anaphylaxis), organ failure, or circulating infection (septic shock). Shock is insidious and can be a hidden killer.

If your cat is in shock, wrap it in a blanket to prevent heat loss.

TIP

If your cat has ever had an episode of anaphylactic shock, discuss with your veterinarian ways that you can help to reduce the risk of a future episode.

LOCAL ALLERGIC REACTIONS

Insect stings and drug reactions sometimes cause a local reaction to your cat's skin rather than the lungs.

When a skin reaction occurs, the affected area is inflamed or swollen, and is itchy, hot, and sometimes painful. Take your cat to the vet as soon as possible if you see any of these symptoms. Your cat will need to be given corticosteroid or noradrenalin by injection immediately, and monitored carefully for any signs of developing anaphylactic shock.

SYMPTOMS OF EARLY STAGES OF SHOCK

In the early stages of shock, a cat has a rapid heartbeat and breathes quickly as its body tries to compensate for the reduction in blood flow. Left untreated, the body will eventually slow down to reduce the effects of injury and illness.

1 Your cat's breathing is faster than normal. Your cat may sometimes pant.

2 Your cat has a pounding pulse or its heart rate is faster than normal.

3 There is a drop in your cat's body temperature.

4 Your cat is in a subdued mental state, which may lead to lethargy or restlessness.

5 When you put finger pressure on the (already pale) gums, the refill time is about two seconds (see pages 20–21).

SYMPTOMS OF LATER STAGES OF SHOCK

If left untreated, shock becomes life-threatening. The body can no longer compensate for blood flow changes, and your cat's body systems may become so overtaxed that they shut down altogether, resulting in the cat's death.

1 Your cat's breathing becomes slow and shallow, and its extremities will feel cool to the touch.

2 Your cat's heart rate slows and becomes irregular.

3 Your cat's gums become pale or blue. Its eyes dilate.

4 Your cat's mental state becomes extremely depressed, eventually leading to unconsciousness.

5 Your cat's pulse becomes weak or absent.

6 When pressed, the cat's gums take over four seconds to refill. **Heart failure and death are imminent.**

TREATING YOUR CAT FOR SHOCK

If your cat is in shock, treat the most urgent problems first. Stem any external bleeding, and give CPR if your cat is not breathing and its heart has stopped. As soon as your cat is stable, go to the veterinary hospital for professional help.

1 Do not give your cat anything to eat or drink, and do not let it wander.

2 Stop any obvious bleeding with finger pressure or, if absolutely necessary, a tourniquet (see pages 48–49).

3 Keep your cat still, and wrap it loosely in a blanket to conserve body heat.

4 Keep your cat's hindquarters elevated with a pillow or towels. This encourages blood to flow to the heart and brain.

5 Give artificial respiration or heart massage as necessary (see pages 34–37).

6 Take your cat to the veterinarian. Ensure that the cat's head is extended during the journey.

ANAPHYLACTIC SHOCK

An insect bite, pollens and other allergens, drugs, or, rarely, a food can cause an allergic reaction and cause a cat to go into anaphylactic shock. A vet is urgently needed to give drugs to counter this life-threatening allergic event.

Has your cat just had an injection or any medication? Has it been stung by an insect? Does it have a history of anaphylaxis?

YES

Is your cat's breathing labored? Is it hiding or crouched, or unwilling to move? Is your cat pawing at its face?

YES

Are your cat's gums blue? Is it showing symptoms of clinical shock?

YES

Your cat may be in anaphylactic shock. Keep its airway open and give artificial respiration (see pages 34–35).

Is your cat making distressed gurgling or wheezing sounds when it tries to breathe?

YES

Your cat's lungs may be filling with liquid. Suspend your cat by its hind legs for 10 seconds to try to clear the airway. See the veterinarian as soon as possible.

ARTIFICIAL RESPIRATION

Your cat's brain craves oxygen; without it for a few minutes permanent brain damage occurs. Give artificial respiration if your cat's heart is still beating, but its breathing has stopped. If its heart has also stopped beating, give artificial respiration and heart massage, together called cardiopulmonary resuscitation (CPR).

    In humans, resuscitation techniques are commonly used to revive stroke and heart-attack patients. Fortunately, these conditions are rare in cats. However, your cat may need these life-saving procedures for other reasons, such as poisoning, choking, smoke inhalation, electrocution, near-drowning, heart failure, concussion, blood loss, shock, or uncontrolled diabetes.

Pinch your cat hard between its toes. If your cat is conscious, it will react automatically by blinking.

Check to see if your cat has a heartbeat. If there is no pulse, begin artificial respiration and heart massage.

IS YOUR CAT CONSCIOUS?

To assess the condition of your cat and determine whether CPR is necessary, follow the steps below.

1 Speak to your cat. If it responds, then your cat is conscious.

2 If your cat does not respond, try pinching it hard between the toes. Carefully watch its eyes. Does your cat blink? If it does, it is conscious.

3 If your cat does not respond to either of the above, try pulling one of its legs. If it resists being pulled, it is conscious. A conscious cat does not need artificial respiration.

4 If your cat fails to respond to any of the above, it is unconscious. Emergency treatment is required.

5 If your cat is not breathing, but it has a heartbeat, give artificial respiration.

6 If your cat's heart and breathing have both stopped, you should also use heart massage (see pages 36–37).

IS YOUR CAT BREATHING?

An unconscious cat sometimes respires so gently that it is difficult to see it breathing. If you are not sure whether your cat is breathing, hold a mirror close to its nose and look for condensation, either fogging or tiny water droplets. If condensation is present, your cat is breathing. Alternatively, hold a small piece of tissue or cotton batting in front of its nostrils. If the material moves, the cat is breathing.

A-B-C

- Think A–B–C. Airway–Breathing–Circulation.
- Is your cat's airway open? If not, clear any debris and pull its tongue forward. Be careful not to get bitten opening its mouth.
- Is your cat breathing? If not, give artificial respiration.
- Does your cat have a heartbeat or pulse? If not, give heart massage.

GIVING ARTIFICIAL RESPIRATION

If your cat has stopped breathing, but its heart is still beating, start to give artificial respiration.

1 Place your cat on its side. Clear away any debris blocking the cat's nose or throat. Pull the cat's tongue forward.

2 Close its mouth. Wrap your hand around your cat's muzzle to make it airtight. Then, blow into its nose until you see its chest expand. Your mouth will seal its nose, mouth, and lips.

3 Take your mouth away and let the cat's lungs deflate naturally.

4 Repeat this procedure 20 to 30 times per minute.

5 Check your cat's pulse every 10 seconds to make sure that its heart is still beating.

6 If your cat's heart should stop, integrate heart massage with artificial respiration (see pages 36–37).

To give artificial respiration, cup your hands around the cat's muzzle and blow gently into its nostrils.

HEART MASSAGE

If a cat's heart stops, heart massage must be administered immediately. You must try to get the heart beating before attempting artificial respiration. To decide what is necessary for your cat, feel for a heartbeat or pulse. Put finger pressure on the cat's gums to squeeze out blood. Does the blanched area refill? If you cannot find a pulse and the gums remain white, you should assume that the heart has stopped. Look at the cat's eyes–they dilate when the heart stops. Integrate heart massage with artificial respiration.

WHAT HAPPENS WHEN A CAT FAINTS?

It can sometimes be difficult to differentiate between fainting and heart failure. A cat faints when there is a reduction in the supply of either oxygen or glucose (sugar) to the brain. Fainting is always temporary. An affected cat recovers consciousness within seconds or minutes. While it is unconscious, the heart continues to beat. Do not give heart massage to a cat that has fainted–you will only cause further damage.

SIGNS OF IMPENDING HEART FAILURE

While there are no absolutely typical signs that tell you that heart failure may occur, watch for any of these signs that may precede heart failure:

- Decreased heart rate
- Blue tongue or gums
- Slow or delayed breathing
- Difficulty in breathing
- Disorientation
- A drop in body temperature to below 99.5° F (37.5° C)

Being realistic, if heart failure does occur, the chances of successfully restarting the heart and overcoming the cause of heart failure are slim.

A cat that has fainted will recover consciousness within a few minutes.

HOW TO GIVE HEART MASSAGE

1 Place your cat on its side, preferably with its head lower than its body. Grasp its chest between your thumb and forefingers, just behind its elbows. Place your other hand on its back.

2 Squeeze your thumb and forefingers firmly together up towards the cat's neck. Be vigorous. Don't worry about bruising your cat, but take care if ribs are obviously broken as they could puncture the heart.

3 Repeat this pumping action at the rate of 100–120 times a minute. Use quick, firm pumps.

4 Administer heart massage for 15 seconds, then give mouth-to-nose artificial respiration for 10 seconds.

5 Check frequently for a pulse. Continue CPR until you feel a pulse. Once it has returned, continue artificial respiration until the cat begins to breathe on its own.

6 Get immediate veterinary attention for your cat.

GIVING CPR WITH TWO PEOPLE

1 One person applies heart massage to the cat for 10 seconds, then stops.

2 The second person immediately gives two breaths into the cat's nose. The first person keeps his or her hands positioned ready for massage.

3 This rhythmical interchange continues until the cat's heart starts to beat.

4 One person continues artificial respiration while the other organizes transport to the vet.

HEART MASSAGE FOR OBESE CATS

1 If your cat is very rotund, place it on its back. Ensure the head is lower than the body.

2 Put the heel of your hand on the cat's breastbone. Press down and forwards to push blood out of the heart to the cat's brain.

3 Continue CPR until heart and breathing resume.

VET'S ADVICE

MORE HELP

If three people are available, one person should elevate the cat's hindquarters and apply pressure to the groin. This directs more blood to the brain, where it is needed most. The other two people should administer CPR.

If your cat's heartbeat has stopped, direct stimulation of the heart may start it beating again.

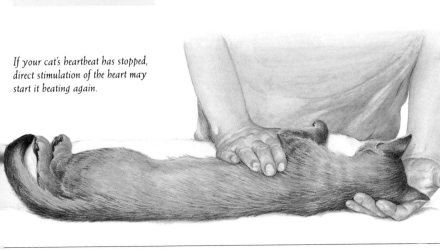

PART 2
SYMPTOMS
CHARTS

For most cat owners, practical veterinary help is
usually only a car-drive away. What is often difficult
is deciding whether your cat's condition justifies the
time and expense involved in a trip to the vet. In many
situations, the need for medical attention is obvious
but the urgency is more difficult to determine. This
section helps you to assess what's happening to your
cat and when you should see your veterinarian.

GENERAL BEHAVIOR

Cats are superb at hiding the fact that they are unwell. In the wild, this is a life-saving strategy for such a small animal. The longer you live with your cat, the better you will become at interpreting what it is telling you through its behavior. Simple behavior changes such as hiding, staring, or acting in a subdued fashion, while not dramatic, may indicate serious, even potentially fatal, conditions such as shock.

Current symptoms

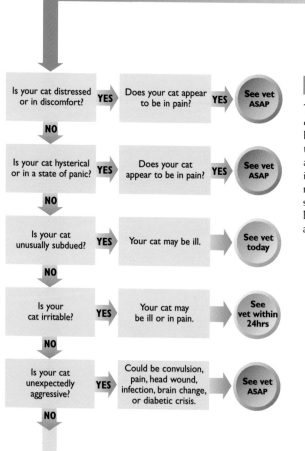

Is your cat distressed or in discomfort?	**YES** → Does your cat appear to be in pain?	**YES** → **See vet ASAP**
NO ↓		
Is your cat hysterical or in a state of panic?	**YES** → Does your cat appear to be in pain?	**YES** → **See vet ASAP**
NO ↓		
Is your cat unusually subdued?	**YES** → Your cat may be ill.	→ **See vet today**
NO ↓		
Is your cat irritable?	**YES** → Your cat may be ill or in pain.	→ **See vet within 24hrs**
NO ↓		
Is your cat unexpectedly aggressive?	**YES** → Could be convulsion, pain, head wound, infection, brain change, or diabetic crisis.	→ **See vet ASAP**
NO ↓		

RABIES

The clinical signs of rabies vary enormously, but all involve behavioral changes. While the typical rabid cat becomes wildly aggressive, spreading the disease in its drooling saliva, other cats may become uncharacteristically subdued. Other signs may include limping, difficulty swallowing, or a paralysis of one or more limbs.

If your normally good-tempered cat suddenly becomes aggressive, it may be unwell.

AGGRESSION

If your cat suddenly becomes aggressive, follow the steps below:

1 Protect yourself, other people, and other animals from bites.

2 Reduce sensory stimulation by eliminating noise and subduing light.

3 Once your cat has become calmer, speak soothingly and observe its response.

4 If your cat has not been vaccinated against rabies and you live in a rabies-endemic area, do not touch your cat. **Call your veterinarian immediately.**

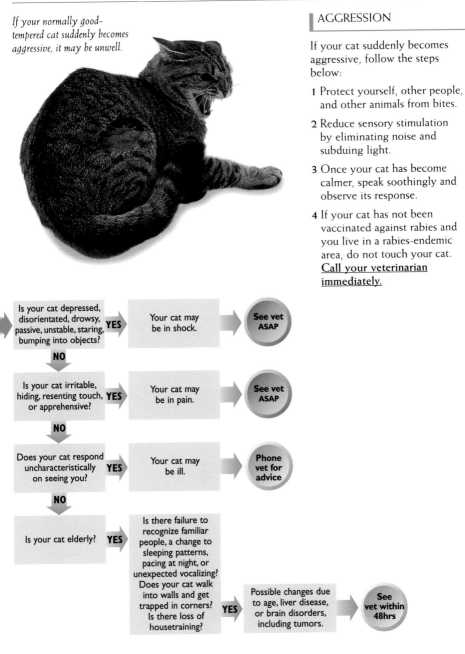

Is your cat depressed, disorientated, drowsy, passive, unstable, staring, bumping into objects? **YES** → Your cat may be in shock. → **See vet ASAP**

NO

Is your cat irritable, hiding, resenting touch, or apprehensive? **YES** → Your cat may be in pain. → **See vet ASAP**

NO

Does your cat respond uncharacteristically on seeing you? **YES** → Your cat may be ill. → **Phone vet for advice**

NO

Is your cat elderly? **YES** → Is there failure to recognize familiar people, a change to sleeping patterns, pacing at night, or unexpected vocalizing? Does your cat walk into walls and get trapped in corners? Is there loss of housetraining? **YES** → Possible changes due to age, liver disease, or brain disorders, including tumors. → **See vet within 48hrs**

LETHARGY

A lack of interest in its owner or surroundings is an important indicator that a cat is unwell. If your cat appears depressed, or is unwilling to move around or play as usual, it may be in pain or suffering from a serious internal disorder. As a general rule, if your cat is suddenly lethargic, see your vet the same day.

Current symptoms

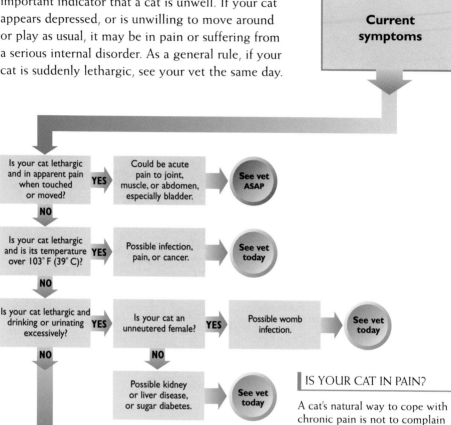

Is your cat lethargic and in apparent pain when touched or moved? **YES** → Could be acute pain to joint, muscle, or abdomen, especially bladder. → **See vet ASAP**

NO

Is your cat lethargic and is its temperature over 103°F (39°C)? **YES** → Possible infection, pain, or cancer. → **See vet today**

NO

Is your cat lethargic and drinking or urinating excessively? **YES** → Is your cat an unneutered female? **YES** → Possible womb infection. → **See vet today**

NO / **NO**

Possible kidney or liver disease, or sugar diabetes. → **See vet today**

Is your cat lethargic and vomiting? Has it got diarrhea? **YES** → Could be inflammation of the gastrointestinal system or pancreas. → **See vet today**

NO

Is your cat lethargic and having difficulty in breathing? **YES** → Possible lung, heart, or chest disease (lung cancer, pneumonia, heart failure, pleurisy). → **See vet ASAP**

NO

IS YOUR CAT IN PAIN?

A cat's natural way to cope with chronic pain is not to complain as some humans are prone to do. Rather, it will behave stoically, to conserve movement and energy. Although cats have a more efficient natural painkilling system than we do, they still feel pain. Pain control is an important part of treatment for physical injuries and other medical conditions.

Although illness is the more common cause of depression, a change in your cat's normal lifestyle may also induce depression.

WHAT IS PSYCHOLOGICAL DEPRESSION?

A psychologically depressed cat has lost interest in life. It is not interested in normal play, normal eating, or normal attention from people. While illness is by far the most common cause of general depression, changes in a cat's lifestyle can induce a state of psychological depression. Loss of routine, such as the departure or death of a family member, may induce psychological depression in a cat.

Psychological depression responds to the same stimuli in cats as it does in people—physical contact, attention, and increased play.

Is your cat lethargic with lameness or limping? **YES**	Possible muscle or joint pain, or fight abscess.	**See vet within 24hrs**

NO

Is your cat lethargic and lacking an appetite? Has it lost weight? **YES**	Could be in pain or possible kidney disease, diabetes, or tumor.	**See vet within 24hrs**

NO

Do you have a lethargic male cat that is straining to urinate? **YES**	Possible blocked bladder.	**See vet ASAP**

NO

Is your cat lethargic with pale gums? **YES**	Do you have any reason to suspect internal or external blood loss? **YES**	Possible trauma, bone marrow disease, cancer, infection, or fluid loss.	**See vet ASAP**

NO

Does your cat's lethargy improve when it eats its food? **YES**	May be low blood sugar due to a number of causes (e.g., liver disease).	**See vet today**

NO

DO CATS SUFFER FROM DEPRESSION?

When a cat looks lethargic we often interpret its behavior to mean it is depressed. Cats do suffer from depression, but if your cat is unwilling to behave in its normal manner, always eliminate veterinary reasons before assuming that there is a psychological problem.

Is your cat lethargic with yellow gums? **YES**	Possible liver disease.	**See vet within 24hrs**

NO

Is your cat lethargic with any other obvious physical or behavioral changes? **YES**	Possible serious illness.	**See vet ASAP**

CHANGES IN SOUND

To help determine what is happening to your cat, listen to the sounds it makes–not only to its voice, but also to any sounds its body makes. The sound of a cat's nails dragging when it walks, for example, may indicate they are overgrown, but it may also be a sign of a joint or nerve condition. Abnormal vocal sounds almost always indicate a serious problem that needs same-day veterinary attention.

Current symptoms

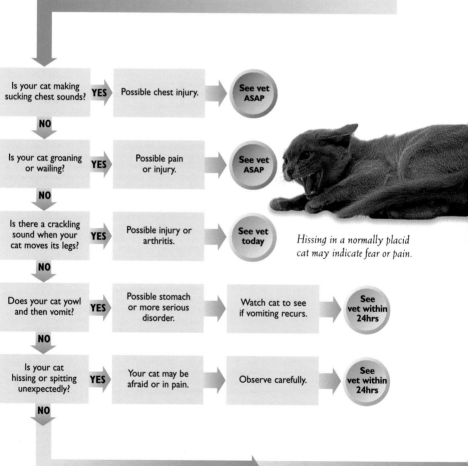

| Is your cat making sucking chest sounds? | **YES** | Possible chest injury. | **See vet ASAP** |

NO

| Is your cat groaning or wailing? | **YES** | Possible pain or injury. | **See vet ASAP** |

NO

| Is there a crackling sound when your cat moves its legs? | **YES** | Possible injury or arthritis. | **See vet today** |

Hissing in a normally placid cat may indicate fear or pain.

NO

| Does your cat yowl and then vomit? | **YES** | Possible stomach or more serious disorder. | Watch cat to see if vomiting recurs. | **See vet within 24hrs** |

NO

| Is your cat hissing or spitting unexpectedly? | **YES** | Your cat may be afraid or in pain. | Observe carefully. | **See vet within 24hrs** |

NO

SOUNDS AND ACTIVITIES

Unusual or changed sounds are often accompanied by changes in your cat's routines and activities. Abnormal sounds accompanied by any of the following changes warrant a veterinary visit within 24 hours:

- Increased restlessness
- Increased sleeping
- Decreased sleeping
- Decreased alertness
- Decreased playfulness

Cats sleep for long periods, but if your cat is sleeping longer than usual, see your vet.

BASIC SOUNDS

Cats make six basic vocal sounds:

- Infantile sound–miaow
- Warning sounds–hiss, spit
- Eliciting sound–chirp
- Pleasure sound–purr
- Calming sound–purr
- Withdrawal sounds–wail, shriek

A change in the use of any of these sounds, especially warning, calming, and withdrawal sounds, is significant and warrants investigating.

PANTING

Do not mistake panting from heat or excitement, which is usually not serious, for labored breathing, which may be serious. If your cat is hot, nervous, excited, or exhausted it will sometimes pant (shallow, rapid, open-mouthed breathing). This is not usually a problem for your veterinarian. Contact your veterinarian if there is inexplicable panting, however, which may be caused by pain, exercise or even some medications, such as corticosteroids.

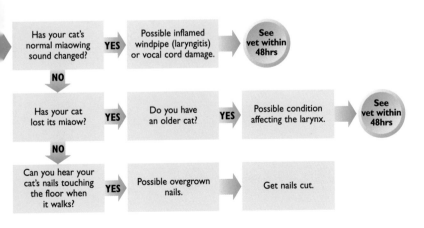

INJURIES

Minor injuries can be treated at home, but be vigilant. Apparently minor surface injuries may be more devastating internally, leading to life-threatening shock. To assess the condition of your cat, run your hands gently over its body. If possible, get another person to restrain your cat; this prevents the cat scratching or biting you. Watch for the following signs of shock: pale gums, a rapid heart rate, or rapid breathing (see pages 32–33). Restlessness and anxiety can develop into weakness and fatigue, while increasingly shallow breathing leads to unconsciousness.

PUNCTURE WOUNDS

Puncture wounds, from fights with other animals, road traffic accidents, pellets, and arrows may appear minor but often are not.

Clean any superficial wounds with salt water (1 teaspoon salt to I cup, 250 ml water) or 3 per cent hydrogen peroxide.

Assume that any puncture wound is infected.

See your veterinarian the same day.

HAIR IN WOUNDS

Hair almost always gets in skin wounds. When cutting hair away from wounds, use a little water-soluble jelly on the scissors. Hair sticks to the jelly. Never use petroleum jelly. It is not water soluble and is difficult to remove later.

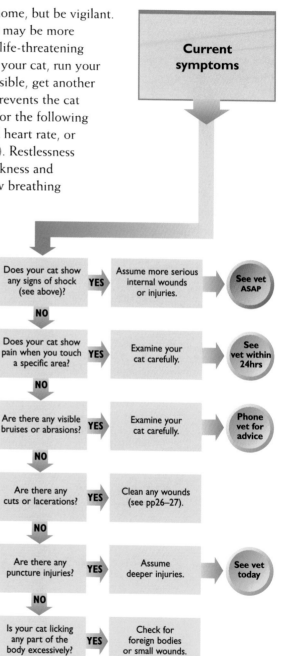

Current symptoms

Does your cat show any signs of shock (see above)? **YES** → Assume more serious internal wounds or injuries. → **See vet ASAP**

NO

Does your cat show pain when you touch a specific area? **YES** → Examine your cat carefully. → **See vet within 24hrs**

NO

Are there any visible bruises or abrasions? **YES** → Examine your cat carefully. → **Phone vet for advice**

NO

Are there any cuts or lacerations? **YES** → Clean any wounds (see pp26–27).

NO

Are there any puncture injuries? **YES** → Assume deeper injuries. → **See vet today**

NO

Is your cat licking any part of the body excessively? **YES** → Check for foreign bodies or small wounds.

INSECT BITES

A cat may have an allergic reaction to an insect bite and go into shock. With this form of shock, known as anaphylactic shock, there is an allergic swelling of the air passages. This causes the cat to make moist, gurgling sounds while trying to breathe. Your cat urgently needs adrenaline by injection to stop anaphylactic shock.

Keep the airway open (see pages 34–35) and get immediate veterinary help.

A bee sting may cause some cats to go into anaphylactic shock.

SNAKE BITES

Snakes (rattlers, copperheads, and cottonmouths in the US, and rattlesnakes in Canada) bite cats much more frequently than they bite people.

The signs of a poisonous snake bite are:

- Trembling
- Excitement
- Vomiting
- Collapse
- Drooling saliva
- Dilated pupils

If your cat is bitten, use a bandage to wrap a cold compress (see page 59) around the affected limb, put your cat in a covered box, and see a local vet as soon as possible.

If your cat is bitten by a snake, it may drool saliva. Seek immediate veterinary help.

EXCESSIVE LICKING

Cats lick their wounds to clean and disinfect them. Some cats lick obsessively, however, which becomes counter-productive because it interferes with the natural healing process.

Other cats appear to lick for no reason, but there is always a cause. Excessive licking is often associated with allergic irritation. Cats may lick so obsessively that it causes partial hair loss and sore patches on the skin.

Licking is a necessary part of a cat's daily grooming routine, but excessive licking may cause irritation.

BLEEDING

External bleeding is simple to monitor. Minor wounds should stop bleeding within five minutes after applying simple pressure. Blood spurting can indicate a cut artery, however, which is often difficult to control. Any wound that bleeds for longer than five minutes needs immediate veterinary attention. Internal bleeding is more difficult to assess and can create a serious emergency.

Current symptoms

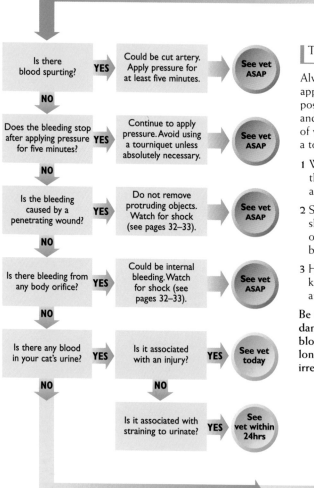

Is there blood spurting?	**YES** → Could be cut artery. Apply pressure for at least five minutes.	→ **See vet ASAP**
NO ↓		
Does the bleeding stop after applying pressure for five minutes?	**YES** → Continue to apply pressure. Avoid using a tourniquet unless absolutely necessary.	→ **See vet ASAP**
NO ↓		
Is the bleeding caused by a penetrating wound?	**YES** → Do not remove protruding objects. Watch for shock (see pages 32–33).	→ **See vet ASAP**
NO ↓		
Is there bleeding from any body orifice?	**YES** → Could be internal bleeding. Watch for shock (see pages 32–33).	→ **See vet ASAP**
NO ↓		
Is there any blood in your cat's urine?	**YES** → Is it associated with an injury? **YES** →	**See vet today**
NO ↓	**NO** ↓	
	Is it associated with straining to urinate? **YES** →	**See vet within 24hrs**

TOURNIQUETS

Always try to stop bleeding by applying pressure. If this is not possible or is not successful, and you are not within reach of veterinary attention, apply a tourniquet to a limb wound.

1 Wrap a piece of fabric above the bleeding wound and tie a knot.

2 Slip a pen, stick, or other firm, slender object into the middle of the knot and twist until the bleeding stops.

3 Hold or tie down the object, keeping the bandage firm and tight.

Be aware that tourniquets are dangerous as they cut off the blood supply. If left on too long, a tourniquet can cause irreversible damage to the limb.

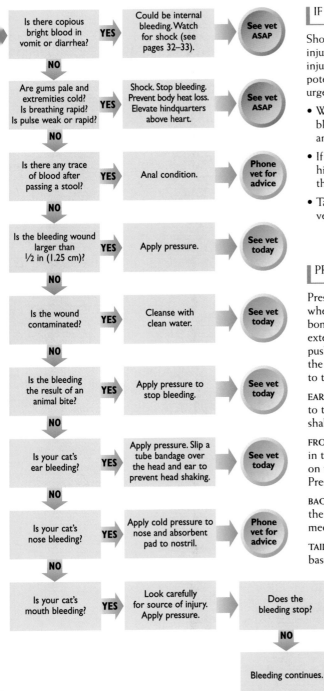

IF SHOCK DEVELOPS

Shock indicates hidden, deeper injuries. Both shock and the injuries that caused it are potentially fatal if not treated urgently (see pages 32–33):

- Wrap your cat in a warm blanket and withhold all food and drink.

- If possible, keep the hindquarters higher than the heart and head.

- Take your cat to the nearest veterinarian immediately.

PRESSURE POINTS

Pressure points are locations where blood vessels travel over bones and can be compressed by external pressure of fingers pushing the blood vessel against the bone. Applying hand pressure to these points stops bleeding.

EAR Apply pressure directly to the wound. Prevent head shaking, which dislodges clots.

FRONT LEG Place three fingers in the armpit and the thumb on the other side of the limb. Press firmly.

BACK LEG Place three fingers in the inner thigh, where the limb meets the body. Press firmly.

TAIL Apply pressure under the base of the tail.

EYE PROBLEMS

Conditions affecting your cat's eyes are not always obvious. Symptoms that appear to be insignificant may indicate potentially devastating conditions. Eye injuries are most often caused by cat fights. For almost all eye conditions, it is best to get veterinary advice. Your vet or a veterinary ophthalmologist can make an accurate diagnosis, using specialist equipment.

Current symptoms

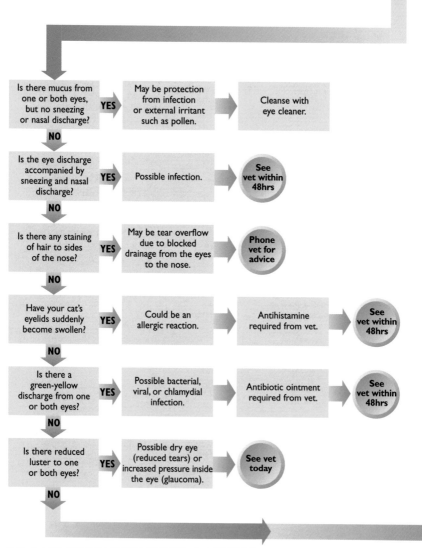

Is there mucus from one or both eyes, but no sneezing or nasal discharge? **YES** → May be protection from infection or external irritant such as pollen. → Cleanse with eye cleaner.

NO

Is the eye discharge accompanied by sneezing and nasal discharge? **YES** → Possible infection. → **See vet within 48hrs**

NO

Is there any staining of hair to sides of the nose? **YES** → May be tear overflow due to blocked drainage from the eyes to the nose. → **Phone vet for advice**

NO

Have your cat's eyelids suddenly become swollen? **YES** → Could be an allergic reaction. → Antihistamine required from vet. → **See vet within 48hrs**

NO

Is there a green-yellow discharge from one or both eyes? **YES** → Possible bacterial, viral, or chlamydial infection. → Antibiotic ointment required from vet. → **See vet within 48hrs**

NO

Is there reduced luster to one or both eyes? **YES** → Possible dry eye (reduced tears) or increased pressure inside the eye (glaucoma). → **See vet today**

NO

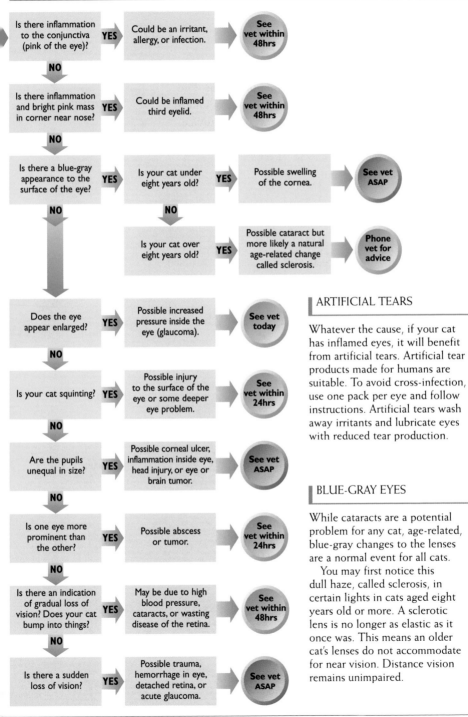

ARTIFICIAL TEARS

Whatever the cause, if your cat has inflamed eyes, it will benefit from artificial tears. Artificial tear products made for humans are suitable. To avoid cross-infection, use one pack per eye and follow instructions. Artificial tears wash away irritants and lubricate eyes with reduced tear production.

BLUE-GRAY EYES

While cataracts are a potential problem for any cat, age-related, blue-gray changes to the lenses are a normal event for all cats.

You may first notice this dull haze, called sclerosis, in certain lights in cats aged eight years old or more. A sclerotic lens is no longer as elastic as it once was. This means an older cat's lenses do not accommodate for near vision. Distance vision remains unimpaired.

EAR PROBLEMS

Most ear injuries in cats are caused by head-to-head cat fights. If an ear is torn by a tooth or a claw in a fight, there is usually little bleeding. However, a bite often leads to hot swelling and a developing abscess, which bursts, usually within five days, discharging foul-smelling pus. Cats may also scratch their ears. This behavior may be part of a general reaction or due to mite infestation.

Current symptoms

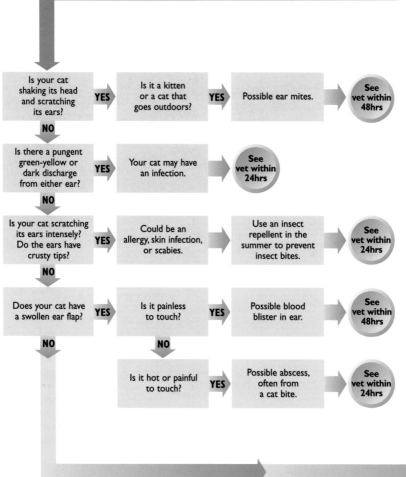

Is your cat shaking its head and scratching its ears? **YES** → Is it a kitten or a cat that goes outdoors? **YES** → Possible ear mites. → **See vet within 48hrs**

NO ↓

Is there a pungent green-yellow or dark discharge from either ear? **YES** → Your cat may have an infection. → **See vet within 24hrs**

NO ↓

Is your cat scratching its ears intensely? Do the ears have crusty tips? **YES** → Could be an allergy, skin infection, or scabies. → Use an insect repellent in the summer to prevent insect bites. → **See vet within 24hrs**

NO ↓

Does your cat have a swollen ear flap? **YES** → Is it painless to touch? **YES** → Possible blood blister in ear. → **See vet within 48hrs**

NO ↓   **NO** ↓

Is it hot or painful to touch? **YES** → Possible abscess, often from a cat bite. → **See vet within 24hrs**

DEAFNESS, AND WHAT TO DO ABOUT IT

Most cats cope well with deafness. If your cat is, or has become, deaf, be patient and try the following:

- Wake your cat with a gentle touch.
- Let it see when you leave.
- If your deaf cat is a kitten, think about getting your pet a feline companion who will act as its ears.

DAMAGE TO THE EARDRUM

The eardrum is a delicate barrier, often damaged by infection or infestation. Once the eardrum has been penetrated, debris accumulates in the middle ear. It is more difficult to clear a middle-ear infection than an external ear infection.

If your cat has recurring ear infections, your vet will examine the eardrum to see if it is ruptured.

ITCHY EARS AND ALLERGY

Vets often see cats with inflamed, itchy ears but the ears themselves are not really the cat's primary problem. The condition of the ears is only the most visible symptom of an underlying problem, which is allergy.

Allergic skin problems often start in the ears, because they are one of the most sensitive and least protected parts of the skin. Treating the root of the condition is essential in preventing a return of the ear problem.

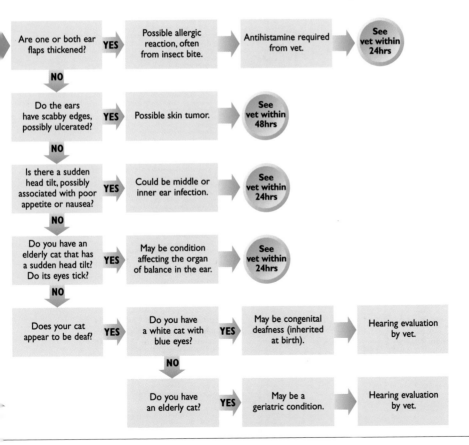

SCRATCHING THE SKIN AND HAIR LOSS

There is always a good reason why a cat scratches or loses its hair, but sometimes it is frustratingly difficult to determine the exact cause. A consequence is that the itching gets treated rather than the actual cause of the itchiness. Parasites and allergy are the most common causes of itchiness in cats. Scratching can often lead to secondary infection.

Current symptoms

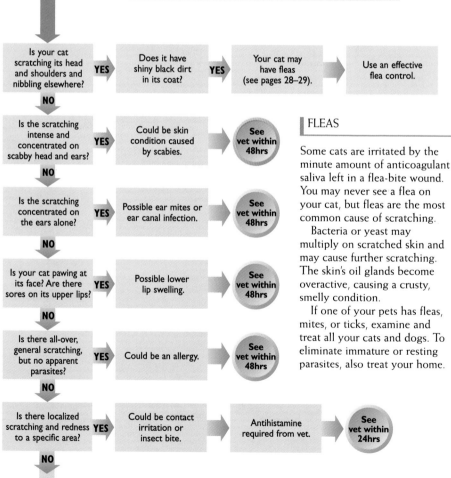

Is your cat scratching its head and shoulders and nibbling elsewhere? — **YES** → Does it have shiny black dirt in its coat? — **YES** → Your cat may have fleas (see pages 28–29). → Use an effective flea control.

NO

Is the scratching intense and concentrated on scabby head and ears? — **YES** → Could be skin condition caused by scabies. → **See vet within 48hrs**

NO

Is the scratching concentrated on the ears alone? — **YES** → Possible ear mites or ear canal infection. → **See vet within 48hrs**

NO

Is your cat pawing at its face? Are there sores on its upper lips? — **YES** → Possible lower lip swelling. → **See vet within 48hrs**

NO

Is there all-over, general scratching, but no apparent parasites? — **YES** → Could be an allergy. → **See vet within 48hrs**

NO

Is there localized scratching and redness to a specific area? — **YES** → Could be contact irritation or insect bite. → Antihistamine required from vet. → **See vet within 24hrs**

NO

FLEAS

Some cats are irritated by the minute amount of anticoagulant saliva left in a flea-bite wound. You may never see a flea on your cat, but fleas are the most common cause of scratching.

Bacteria or yeast may multiply on scratched skin and may cause further scratching. The skin's oil glands become overactive, causing a crusty, smelly condition.

If one of your pets has fleas, mites, or ticks, examine and treat all your cats and dogs. To eliminate immature or resting parasites, also treat your home.

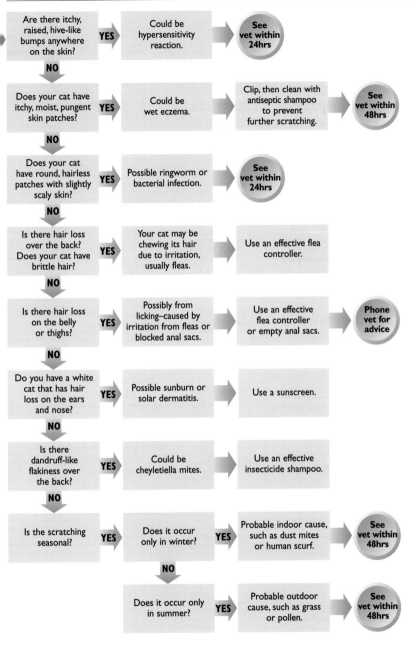

Are there itchy, raised, hive-like bumps anywhere on the skin? **YES** → Could be hypersensitivity reaction. → **See vet within 24hrs**

NO ↓

Does your cat have itchy, moist, pungent skin patches? **YES** → Could be wet eczema. → Clip, then clean with antiseptic shampoo to prevent further scratching. → **See vet within 48hrs**

NO ↓

Does your cat have round, hairless patches with slightly scaly skin? **YES** → Possible ringworm or bacterial infection. → **See vet within 24hrs**

NO ↓

Is there hair loss over the back? Does your cat have brittle hair? **YES** → Your cat may be chewing its hair due to irritation, usually fleas. → Use an effective flea controller.

NO ↓

Is there hair loss on the belly or thighs? **YES** → Possibly from licking—caused by irritation from fleas or blocked anal sacs. → Use an effective flea controller or empty anal sacs. → **Phone vet for advice**

NO ↓

Do you have a white cat that has hair loss on the ears and nose? **YES** → Possible sunburn or solar dermatitis. → Use a sunscreen.

NO ↓

Is there dandruff-like flakiness over the back? **YES** → Could be cheyletiella mites. → Use an effective insecticide shampoo.

NO ↓

Is the scratching seasonal? **YES** → Does it occur only in winter? **YES** → Probable indoor cause, such as dust mites or human scurf. → **See vet within 48hrs**

NO ↓

Does it occur only in summer? **YES** → Probable outdoor cause, such as grass or pollen. → **See vet within 48hrs**

SWELLINGS AND LUMPS

The most common cause of a swelling under a cat's skin is an abscess from an injury, often the result of a cat fight. Abscesses most commonly occur on the head or near the base of the tail. The most common lumps are mammary tumors. These occur under the skin of the chest and belly. Any lump should always be examined by your veterinarian.

Current symptoms

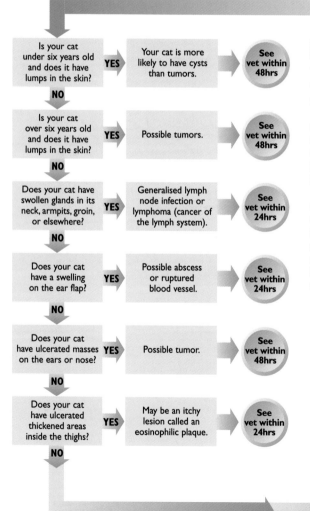

Is your cat under six years old and does it have lumps in the skin?	**YES** Your cat is more likely to have cysts than tumors.	See vet within 48hrs
NO		
Is your cat over six years old and does it have lumps in the skin?	**YES** Possible tumors.	See vet within 48hrs
NO		
Does your cat have swollen glands in its neck, armpits, groin, or elsewhere?	**YES** Generalised lymph node infection or lymphoma (cancer of the lymph system).	See vet within 24hrs
NO		
Does your cat have a swelling on the ear flap?	**YES** Possible abscess or ruptured blood vessel.	See vet within 24hrs
NO		
Does your cat have ulcerated masses on the ears or nose?	**YES** Possible tumor.	See vet within 48hrs
NO		
Does your cat have ulcerated thickened areas inside the thighs?	**YES** May be an itchy lesion called an eosinophilic plaque.	See vet within 24hrs
NO		

AN ACCURATE DIAGNOSIS

Your vet makes an educated guess when he or she feels a lump and makes a diagnosis.

A vet's diagnosis is based on your cat's age, sex, and breed as well as its veterinary history, the location and texture of the lump, and the speed at which it is growing.

With experience, this type of diagnosis is very accurate, but the only definite diagnosis comes from a pathologist, who looks at a biopsy sample under a microscope. Taking a skin biopsy is simple and often does not even require the cat to be sedated.

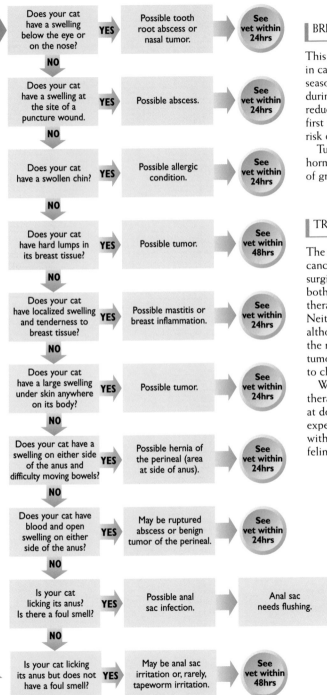

BREAST CANCER

This is the most common cancer in cats. Spaying before the first season eliminates risk. Spaying during the first two years of life reduces risk. Spaying after the first two years does not affect the risk of developing breast cancer.

Tumors feed on female hormones, and they have a surge of growth after each estrus cycle.

TREATMENT FOR CANCER

The most effective way to treat cancer is to remove the lump surgically. If this is not possible, both chemotherapy and radiation therapy are sometimes used. Neither is as effective as surgery, although lymphoma, one of the most common of feline tumors, often responds well to chemotherapy.

When either of these therapies is used, it is employed at doses so that a cat does not experience side effects. Infection with FeLV is often implicated in feline cancers.

LAMENESS AND LIMPING

Lameness may be caused by something as simple as a bite or a bruise, or as significant as a broken bone. Back pain may also cause your cat to limp. A cat with back pain is reluctant to jump up or down, and often walks with a slightly arched back. If your cat is lame, examine the affected limb. Start at the paw and work up the affected leg, feeling for heat, swelling, or dry, matted hair over a puncture wound. Take care: if your examination hurts your cat, you risk being bitten. The best therapy for most minor causes of lameness is rest.

Current symptoms

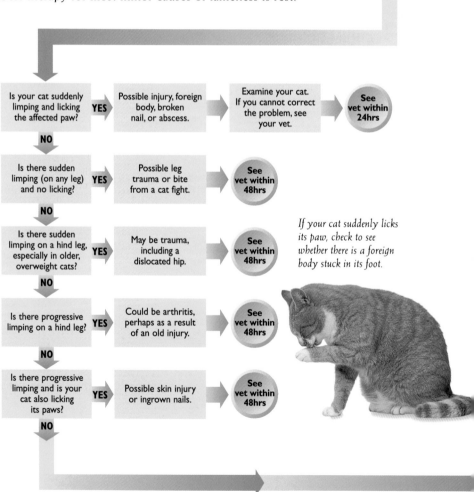

Is your cat suddenly limping and licking the affected paw? **YES** → Possible injury, foreign body, broken nail, or abscess. → Examine your cat. If you cannot correct the problem, see your vet. → **See vet within 24hrs**

NO

Is there sudden limping (on any leg) and no licking? **YES** → Possible leg trauma or bite from a cat fight. → **See vet within 48hrs**

NO

Is there sudden limping on a hind leg, especially in older, overweight cats? **YES** → May be trauma, including a dislocated hip. → **See vet within 48hrs**

NO

Is there progressive limping on a hind leg? **YES** → Could be arthritis, perhaps as a result of an old injury. → **See vet within 48hrs**

NO

Is there progressive limping and is your cat also licking its paws? **YES** → Possible skin injury or ingrown nails. → **See vet within 48hrs**

NO

If your cat suddenly licks its paw, check to see whether there is a foreign body stuck in its foot.

OVERGROWN CLAWS

Overgrown claws are not uncommon in older cats. Left unattended, a long claw may penetrate the associated pad, causing pain, infection, and lameness. Check your cat's claws and clip them routinely. If you are unsure how to clip them safely, your veterinarian will show you the correct method.

TOXIC PAINKILLERS

Never give aspirin, acetaminophen, or ibuprofen to your cat unless told to do so by your veterinarian. All these drugs remain in the cat's system considerably longer than in ours, for days rather than hours. All these painkillers are potentially lethal to a cat.

Aspirin, however, is used therapeutically for certain heart and blood clot disorders. The usual maximum dose is one quarter of an adult human's

Overgrown nails can cause your cat to limp. Ask your veterinarian to show you how to trim them.

COLD COMPRESSES

Strains and sprains benefit from cold compresses, applied three or four times daily. A small bag of frozen peas makes a practical and moldable cold compress. Place a cotton towel over the affected area (this prevents the area freezing), then the frozen bag. Leave in place for 10–15 minutes.

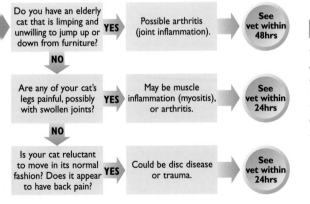

Do you have an elderly cat that is limping and unwilling to jump up or down from furniture? **YES** → Possible arthritis (joint inflammation). → See vet within 48hrs

NO ↓

Are any of your cat's legs painful, possibly with swollen joints? **YES** → May be muscle inflammation (myositis), or arthritis. → See vet within 24hrs

NO ↓

Is your cat reluctant to move in its normal fashion? Does it appear to have back pain? **YES** → Could be disc disease or trauma. → See vet within 24hrs

LOSS OF BALANCE AND COORDINATION

Balance is controlled by the organ of balance in the inner ear and the part of the brain called the cerebellum. Injuries, infections, inflammations, and tumors can affect how a cat stands and walks, as can certain drugs. A head tilt usually indicates a problem in the inner ear, not a stroke. Strokes are less common in cats than in people.

Current symptoms

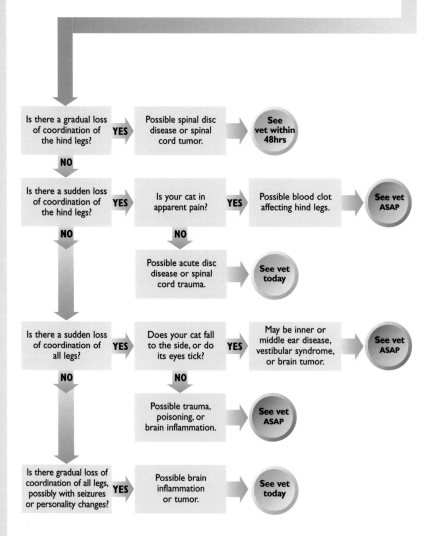

Is there a gradual loss of coordination of the hind legs? **YES** → Possible spinal disc disease or spinal cord tumor. → See vet within 48hrs

NO

Is there a sudden loss of coordination of the hind legs? **YES** → Is your cat in apparent pain? **YES** → Possible blood clot affecting hind legs. → See vet ASAP

NO   **NO**

Possible acute disc disease or spinal cord trauma. → See vet today

Is there a sudden loss of coordination of all legs? **YES** → Does your cat fall to the side, or do its eyes tick? **YES** → May be inner or middle ear disease, vestibular syndrome, or brain tumor. → See vet ASAP

NO   **NO**

Possible trauma, poisoning, or brain inflammation. → See vet ASAP

Is there gradual loss of coordination of all legs, possibly with seizures or personality changes? **YES** → Possible brain inflammation or tumor. → See vet today

SIGNS OF LOSS OF BALANCE

The signs of loss of balance include:

• Walking abnormally or falling down

• Circling in one specific direction

• A drunken appearance

• Head tilting to one side

• Rhythmic flicking of the eyeballs

• Vomiting

Monitor the way your cat walks for any signs of loss of balance or coordination.

OTHER CAUSES OF LOSS OF BALANCE

Any condition that weakens your cat, for example, severe vomiting or diarrhea, may cause a loss of balance. So, too, will chronic joint pain. Stumbling is often worst when a cat first gets up. A loss of vision will also cause a cat to appear to lose balance.

All of these conditions demand veterinary attention and advice.

STROKES

Although strokes are rare in cats, they occur more commonly than once thought. The consequences of a stroke vary according to where the blood clot or hemorrhage occurs in the brain. A stroke may be associated with high blood pressure, which in turn is associated with an overactive thyroid gland and heart disease.

If you suspect poisoning, take your cat and the toxic substance, together with its packaging, to the vet immediately.

POISONING

If poisoning is suspected, collect what you think your cat has consumed and take it and its packaging to your vet, along with your cat. For advice call the ASPCA's National Animal Poison Control Center. Tel: 800-548-2423. A charge is made for this service.

SEIZURES AND CONVULSIONS

At the onset of a seizure, a cat may appear confused, lose balance, or behave erratically. These symptoms often develop into a fit, during which a cat may become rigid, paddle its legs, have tremors, urinate, defecate, or salivate. Some cats lose consciousness. An episode usually ends within minutes. Affected cats emerge disorientated, seeking solitude, and often hungry. Fortunately seizures are uncommon in cats.

Current symptoms

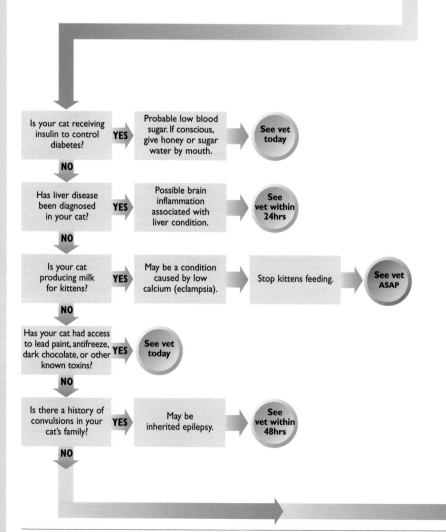

Is your cat receiving insulin to control diabetes? **YES** → Probable low blood sugar. If conscious, give honey or sugar water by mouth. → **See vet today**

NO

Has liver disease been diagnosed in your cat? **YES** → Possible brain inflammation associated with liver condition. → **See vet within 24hrs**

NO

Is your cat producing milk for kittens? **YES** → May be a condition caused by low calcium (eclampsia). → Stop kittens feeding. → **See vet ASAP**

NO

Has your cat had access to lead paint, antifreeze, dark chocolate, or other known toxins? **YES** → **See vet today**

NO

Is there a history of convulsions in your cat's family? **YES** → May be inherited epilepsy. → **See vet within 48hrs**

NO

COMA

A cat that is breathing and appears to be asleep, but does not respond to voice or touch, is in a coma. Comas are most common in diabetic cats, but can also be caused by extremes of temperature, certain drugs, poisons, severe infections, and shock.
ACTION Assess the possible cause of the coma and take your cat to a veterinarian immediately.

SEIZURES IN CATS RECEIVING INSULIN

Excess insulin reduces blood sugar. At first an affected cat appears weak and confused, and may stagger. This quickly develops into sudden seizures or convulsions, sometimes accompanied by profuse salivating.

Give honey, corn syrup, or sugar water at the first sign of weakness or confusion, and see your vet as soon as possible. Do not attempt to give anything orally to an unconscious cat or one that is having a fit.

Has the fit stopped spontaneously within four minutes?	YES → See vet today
NO ↓	
Are fits occurring in clusters?	YES → See vet ASAP

CAUSES OF SEIZURES

Causes from outside the nervous system include:

- Liver disease
- Kidney failure
- Toxins from plants, animals, and chemicals

Causes from inside the nervous system include:

- Bacterial, viral, fungal, or parasitic brain infection
- Brain inflammation
- Brain abscess
- Brain tumor
- Brain scar tissue after a head injury
- Inherited brain abnormalities (birth defects)

WHEN A SEIZURE OCCURS

1 Surround your cat with soft material, cushions, or blankets.

2 Reduce sound and light. Speak quietly and reassuringly.

3 Monitor how long the fit lasts. If a fit lasts more than four minutes, visit your veterinarian as soon as possible.

4 A cat rarely chokes on its tongue. Avoid putting your fingers into your cat's mouth to pull out the tongue unless absolutely necessary.

Your cat's convulsion may be caused by ingesting toxins from other prey animals.

SNEEZING AND NASAL DISORDERS

Sneezing is not an illness—it is a reflex action to rid the nasal passages of something the body considers to be irritating. The most common cause of sneezing, with or without nasal discharge, is infection. Allergy is another increasingly common cause of sneezing in cats. A cat's healthy, slightly moist nose is also prone to injury from head-to-head feline combat.

Current symptoms

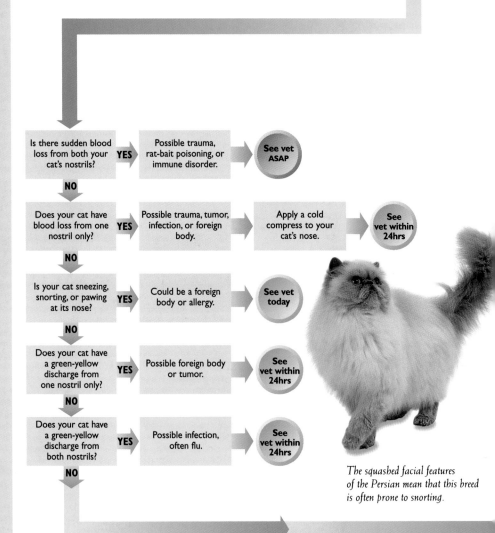

Is there sudden blood loss from both your cat's nostrils? **YES** → Possible trauma, rat-bait poisoning, or immune disorder. → **See vet ASAP**

NO ↓

Does your cat have blood loss from one nostril only? **YES** → Possible trauma, tumor, infection, or foreign body. → Apply a cold compress to your cat's nose. → **See vet within 24hrs**

NO ↓

Is your cat sneezing, snorting, or pawing at its nose? **YES** → Could be a foreign body or allergy. → **See vet today**

NO ↓

Does your cat have a green-yellow discharge from one nostril only? **YES** → Possible foreign body or tumor. → **See vet within 24hrs**

NO ↓

Does your cat have a green-yellow discharge from both nostrils? **YES** → Possible infection, often flu. → **See vet within 24hrs**

NO ↓

The squashed facial features of the Persian mean that this breed is often prone to snorting.

NOSE BLEEDS

If your cat's nose bleeds, DO the following:

• Keep your cat quiet and confined.

• Apply a cold compress to the top of the nose for five minutes. A packet of frozen peas wrapped in plastic wrap makes an ideal cold compress.

• Cover the bleeding nostril with absorbent material.

• Seek veterinary attention the same day.

DO NOT do the following:

• Do not tilt your cat's head back to prevent blood dripping.

• Do not pack the bleeding nostril with anything. This will only stimulate sneezing.

FOREIGN OBJECTS IN THE NOSE

If you can see an object, such as a blade of grass or a seed, in your cat's nostrils, carefully remove it with tweezers. If you are unable to remove the object easily, get veterinary help immediately.

SINUSITIS

Infection to the sinuses produces a constant flow of discharge through the nasal passages. This often creates outbursts of sneezing, accompanied by copious amounts of green-yellow material. There may be an associated eye inflammation (conjunctivitis). Sinusitis is very difficult to control without the use of long-term antibiotic therapy

An unusual form of sinusitis is caused by the fungus *cryptococcus*, found in bird droppings. Sometimes called pigeon fancier's disease, *cryptococcus* is a serious health risk to cats with immune system disorders.

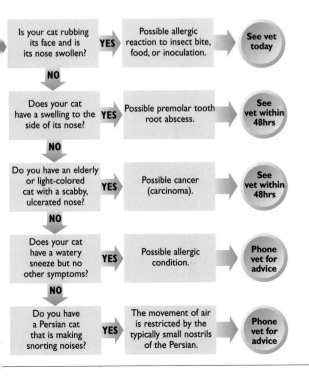

COUGHING, CHOKING, AND GAGGING

Coughing is caused by irritation to the lungs or windpipe. Gagging is caused by throat irritation. Choking occurs when, for any reason, the windpipe is blocked. Choking is an immediate emergency. Do not wait for veterinary help. Try to remove the cause of the choking, but be careful—a choking cat is in great distress and liable to scratch and bite.

Current symptoms: coughing	Current symptoms: gagging

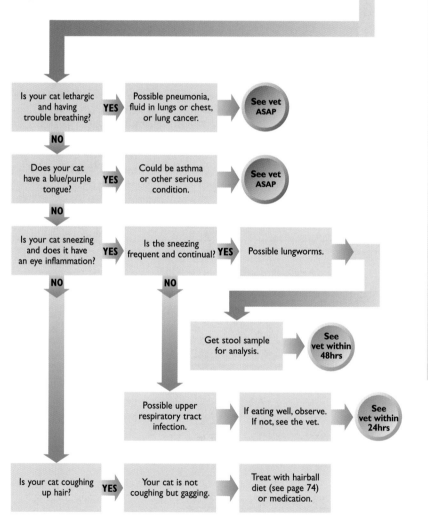

Is your cat lethargic and having trouble breathing? **YES** → Possible pneumonia, fluid in lungs or chest, or lung cancer. → **See vet ASAP**

NO

Does your cat have a blue/purple tongue? **YES** → Could be asthma or other serious condition. → **See vet ASAP**

NO

Is your cat sneezing and does it have an eye inflammation? **YES** → Is the sneezing frequent and continual? **YES** → Possible lungworms. →

NO — **NO**

Get stool sample for analysis. → **See vet within 48hrs**

Possible upper respiratory tract infection. → If eating well, observe. If not, see the vet. → **See vet within 24hrs**

Is your cat coughing up hair? **YES** → Your cat is not coughing but gagging. → Treat with hairball diet (see page 74) or medication.

OBJECT IN MOUTH OF CONSCIOUS CAT

1 Restrain cat by wrapping its body in a bulky towel or other available material.

2 From above, grasp the upper jaw, and press the upper lips over the upper teeth.

3 With your other hand, pull down the lower jaw. Push the cheeks between teeth with the first hand.

4 Using a spoon handle, remove object stuck on the teeth or in roof of the mouth. Take care not to let object fall back into the throat.

CONSCIOUS AND CHOKING

1 Put your cat on its side with its back towards you. With the palm of your hand, press firmly up and forwards, just behind the rib cage.

2 Alternatively, place both hands on either side of the belly and squeeze firmly up and forwards.

PREVENT CHOKING

Cats can choke on a variety of objects. Bone may cause a problem if it gets stuck in the teeth at the back of the mouth. Prevent this by keeping your rubbish in covered containers.

Cats love playing with thread. Always tidy up thoroughly after sewing. If you see thread hanging from your cat's mouth, pull gently on it. If it does not come out, do not pull more or cut it. See your vet immediately.

UNCONSCIOUS FROM CHOKING

1 With the cat on its side, place the heel of your hand just behind the cat's back ribs.

2 Press sharply to expel the blockage.

3 Taking care, use your finger to sweep any debris from the cat's mouth.

4 If necessary, give artificial respiration and heart massage (CPR, see pages 34–35).

5 If CPR is necessary, get immediate veterinary assistance for your cat.

OTHER CAUSES OF CHOKING

Physical injuries to the neck or throat may cause swelling and choking. An allergic reaction to an insect bite or sting in the mouth may cause the tongue to swell. A cat may also choke on its own vomit.

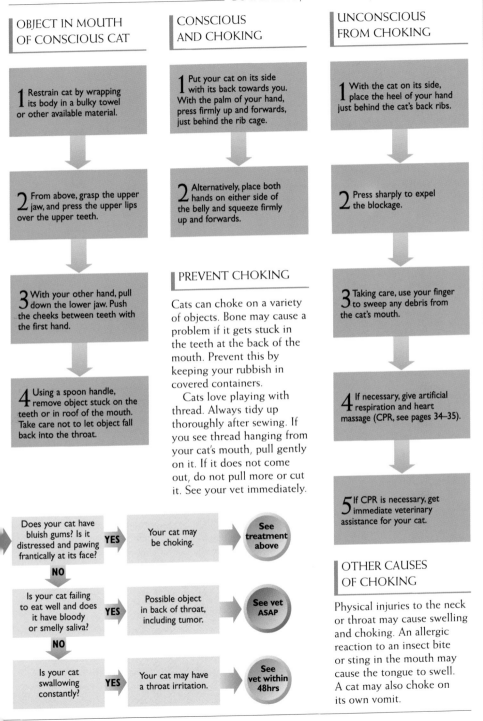

Does your cat have bluish gums? Is it distressed and pawing frantically at its face? **YES** → Your cat may be choking. → **See treatment above**

NO

Is your cat failing to eat well and does it have bloody or smelly saliva? **YES** → Possible object in back of throat, including tumor. → **See vet ASAP**

NO

Is your cat swallowing constantly? **YES** → Your cat may have a throat irritation. → **See vet within 48hrs**

BAD BREATH

Bad breath, or halitosis, is most often caused by poor oral hygiene and the build-up of bacteria associated with excessive tartar on the teeth. It may also be caused by mouth infections and, in older cats, mouth tumors. Bad breath may also be a sign of more serious problems, including sugar diabetes, kidney disease, and a range of digestive disorders.

Current symptoms

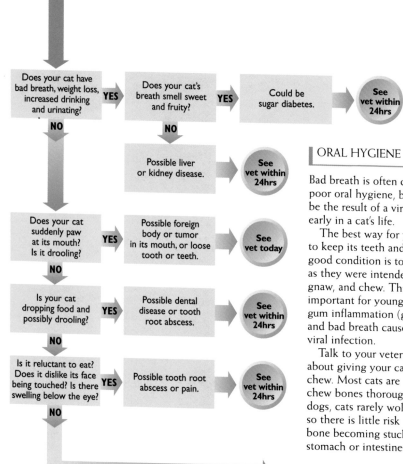

Does your cat have bad breath, weight loss, increased drinking and urinating? — **YES** → Does your cat's breath smell sweet and fruity? — **YES** → Could be sugar diabetes. → **See vet within 24hrs**

NO ↓ (from breath sweet) → Possible liver or kidney disease. → **See vet within 24hrs**

NO ↓

Does your cat suddenly paw at its mouth? Is it drooling? — **YES** → Possible foreign body or tumor in its mouth, or loose tooth or teeth. → **See vet today**

NO ↓

Is your cat dropping food and possibly drooling? — **YES** → Possible dental disease or tooth root abscess. → **See vet within 24hrs**

NO ↓

Is it reluctant to eat? Does it dislike its face being touched? Is there swelling below the eye? — **YES** → Possible tooth root abscess or pain. → **See vet within 24hrs**

NO ↓

ORAL HYGIENE

Bad breath is often caused by poor oral hygiene, but it may also be the result of a viral infection early in a cat's life.

The best way for your cat to keep its teeth and gums in good condition is to use them as they were intended–to tear, gnaw, and chew. This is vitally important for young cats with gum inflammation (gingivitis) and bad breath caused by a viral infection.

Talk to your veterinarian about giving your cat bones to chew. Most cats are sensible and chew bones thoroughly. Unlike dogs, cats rarely wolf bone down so there is little risk of food or bone becoming stuck in the stomach or intestines.

ORAL TUMORS

Oral tumors are, regrettably, not uncommon in older cats. These may occur on the tongue, in the jaw, or in the roof of the mouth. Jaw tumors must be differentiated from jawbone infection, which occurs as a result of untreated tooth root infection. Any mouth swelling and bad breath should be investigated immediately by your vet.

Teething kittens may have temporary bad breath, which will soon pass.

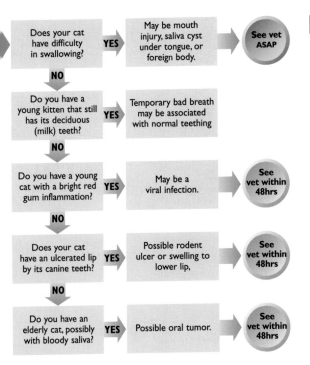

EXCESSIVE DRIBBLING

Cats are great dribblers, often for minor reasons. Anything that tastes unpleasant, such as medicines, some foods, or common household products, may produce a virtual waterfall of saliva. Excess dribbling may also be associated with motion sickness. More seriously, poisons affecting the nervous system, mouth disorders, gastrointestinal ailments, and metabolic conditions such as kidney failure may cause excessive dribbling. If your cat is drooling excessively and you do not know why, contact your veterinarian immediately.

Does your cat have difficulty in swallowing? **YES** May be mouth injury, saliva cyst under tongue, or foreign body. → **See vet ASAP**

NO

Do you have a young kitten that still has its deciduous (milk) teeth? **YES** Temporary bad breath may be associated with normal teething.

NO

Do you have a young cat with a bright red gum inflammation? **YES** May be a viral infection. → **See vet within 48hrs**

NO

Does your cat have an ulcerated lip by its canine teeth? **YES** Possible rodent ulcer or swelling to lower lip, → **See vet within 48hrs**

NO

Do you have an elderly cat, possibly with bloody saliva? **YES** Possible oral tumor. → **See vet within 48hrs**

BREATHING PROBLEMS

With most breathing problems, your cat will use its stomach muscles increasingly to get in more air. Respiratory problems involving the windpipe and lungs are usually obvious. However, breathing problems associated with a build-up of fluid in the chest or abdomen may develop more insidiously. These can be more serious, often being caused by injury, heart or liver disease, or potentially lethal viral infections.

Current symptoms

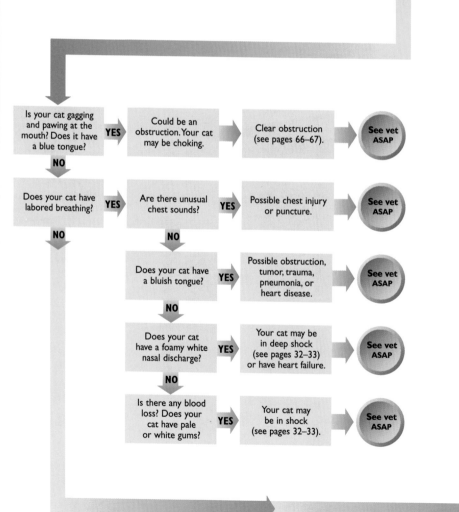

Is your cat gagging and pawing at the mouth? Does it have a blue tongue? **YES** → Could be an obstruction. Your cat may be choking. → Clear obstruction (see pages 66–67). → **See vet ASAP**

NO

Does your cat have labored breathing? **YES** → Are there unusual chest sounds? **YES** → Possible chest injury or puncture. → **See vet ASAP**

NO — **NO**

Does your cat have a bluish tongue? **YES** → Possible obstruction, tumor, trauma, pneumonia, or heart disease. → **See vet ASAP**

NO

Does your cat have a foamy white nasal discharge? **YES** → Your cat may be in deep shock (see pages 32–33) or have heart failure. → **See vet ASAP**

NO

Is there any blood loss? Does your cat have pale or white gums? **YES** → Your cat may be in shock (see pages 32–33). → **See vet ASAP**

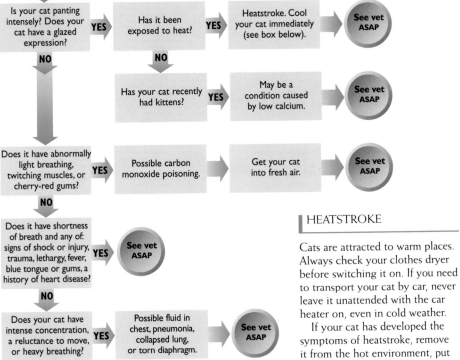

WHEEZING

Wheezing means there is a lung problem, an inflammation to the air passages (bronchitis). It is usually caused by allergy, but can also be caused by infection.

Asthma in cats is very similar to asthma in people. It can be just as dangerous, but fortunately responds to the same medications that we use.

A wheeze can develop into shock. If your cat is wheezing, see your vet the same day.

HEATSTROKE

Cats are attracted to warm places. Always check your clothes dryer before switching it on. If you need to transport your cat by car, never leave it unattended with the car heater on, even in cold weather.

If your cat has developed the symptoms of heatstroke, remove it from the hot environment, put it in a sink or bath, and run water over the cat, especially over its head, allowing water to fill the sink. Alternatively, place your cat in a pool of water or hose it thoroughly. A packet of frozen vegetables placed on its head will help it cool down.

CHANGES IN APPETITE

Cats enjoy routine, including eating routines. A simple change of cat-food brand may be accompanied by a change of appetite. While some cats are always hungry, an increased appetite in a cat may be a sign of an overactive thyroid gland. A decrease in appetite almost always warrants contacting your veterinarian.

Current symptoms

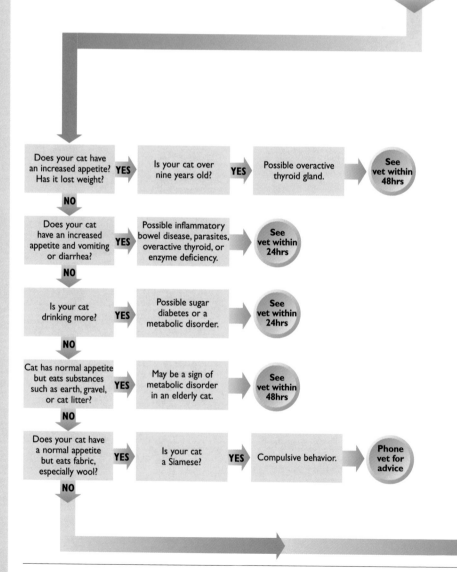

Does your cat have an increased appetite? Has it lost weight? **YES** → Is your cat over nine years old? **YES** → Possible overactive thyroid gland. → **See vet within 48hrs**

NO

Does your cat have an increased appetite and vomiting or diarrhea? **YES** → Possible inflammatory bowel disease, parasites, overactive thyroid, or enzyme deficiency. → **See vet within 24hrs**

NO

Is your cat drinking more? **YES** → Possible sugar diabetes or a metabolic disorder. → **See vet within 24hrs**

NO

Cat has normal appetite but eats substances such as earth, gravel, or cat litter? **YES** → May be a sign of metabolic disorder in an elderly cat. → **See vet within 48hrs**

NO

Does your cat have a normal appetite but eats fabric, especially wool? **YES** → Is your cat a Siamese? **YES** → Compulsive behavior. → **Phone vet for advice**

NO

MULTIPLE CAT HOUSEHOLDS

If one cat grows fat and another remains at its normal size in a multiple-cat household, monitor how much each cat is eating. It is not uncommon for one individual to eat the majority of the food. If this is happening, and weight gain has become a veterinary problem, the only effective solution is to monitor your cats as they eat. Never leave uneaten food in their dishes.

HOW MEDICINES AFFECT THE APPETITE

If your cat is being treated with any medicine, ask your veterinarian if the medicine may have any effects on appetite. Some medications, such as corticosteroids, increase hunger, sometimes quite dramatically. Other medications, such as some antibiotics, may cause a temporary reduction, or even loss, of appetite.

OUTDOOR CATS GAINING WEIGHT

If your outdoor cat gains weight, it may have found a new source of food, such as wildlife, refuse, or a neighbor who provides routine handouts. Some inventive cats lead double lives, living with two families. Modify feeding according to how much your cat eats, regardless of where the food is coming from.

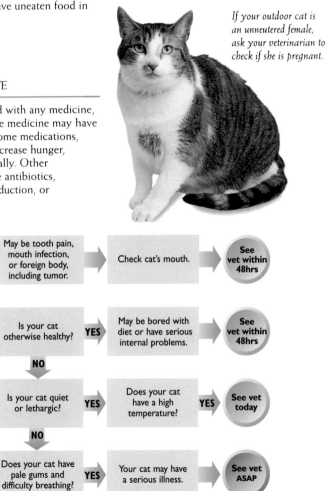

If your outdoor cat is an unneutered female, ask your veterinarian to check if she is pregnant.

Does your cat have a normal desire to eat but then becomes picky?	**YES** → May be tooth pain, mouth infection, or foreign body, including tumor.	→ Check cat's mouth.	→ **See vet within 48hrs**

NO ↓

Does your cat have a decreased appetite?	**YES** → Is your cat otherwise healthy?	**YES** → May be bored with diet or have serious internal problems.	→ **See vet within 48hrs**

NO ↓

	Is your cat quiet or lethargic?	**YES** → Does your cat have a high temperature?	**YES** → **See vet today**

NO ↓

Does your cat have pale gums and difficulty breathing?	**YES** → Your cat may have a serious illness.	→ **See vet ASAP**

VOMITING

Vomiting may be caused directly by problems in the gastrointestinal system or indirectly as a result of conditions elsewhere in the body. Lip licking, lip smacking, drooling, swallowing, and gulping are all signs of nausea and can precede vomiting. Regurgitating food covered by mucus indicates a problem with the esophagus, and is not the same as vomiting.

Current symptoms

Do you have a kitten with acute vomiting? **YES** → Possible roundworms or other conditions. → **See vet within 24hrs**

NO

Does your cat eat houseplants or grass, or hunt and eat prey? **YES** → Possible irritation. → **Phone vet for advice**

NO

Does your cat pass tube-like vomit that contains hair? **YES** → Possible hairballs. → Feed hairball diet or use hairball medication.

NO

Does your cat vomit two or three times weekly? **YES** → **Phone vet for advice**

NO

Is there fresh blood in the vomit? **YES** → **See vet within 24hrs**

NO

Is the vomiting projectile and black, or non-projectile and continuous? **YES** → Possible obstruction, severe intestinal parasites, kidney or liver disease, metabolic disorder, ulcer, tumor, foreign body, bleeding disorder, or drug reaction. → **See vet today**

NO

HAIRBALL DIET

Many cat-food manufacturers produce specially formulated diets for long-haired cats to help them pass any hair swallowed while grooming. These are usually called hairball diets.

A cat may irritate its digestive system by eating grass, causing it to vomit.

SIGNS OF NAUSEA

Nausea usually precedes vomiting. An affected cat loses interest in food and may drool saliva. Vomiting may be preceded by a loud yowl. Simple vomiting is not an emergency. Reduce risks by grooming your cat daily and do not change your cat's diet abruptly. Vomiting associated with straining to urinate, severe diarrhea, or swallowing ribbon or string is an emergency requiring same-day veterinary attention.

WATCH FOR SHOCK

The signs of shock are:
- Pale or white gums
- Rapid heartbeat, double the normal rate
- Fast breathing, over 30 breaths per minute
- Restlessness leading to weakness

TREATMENT FOR SIMPLE VOMITING

1 Take away food and reduce water intake.

2 After six to eight hours, offer your cat one to three teaspoons of regular or bland food such as chicken and rice.

3 After six to eight hours, permit more drinking–give small amounts often.

4 If no further vomiting, offer more food every two hours. Return to regular diet next day.

5 If your cat is dehydrated, in shock, or has other conditions, treat for shock (see pages 32–33) and see your veterinarian immediately.

Never withhold food from a young kitten, as this could lead to a dangerous drop in blood sugar level. If your kitten starts vomiting, call your vet for advice.

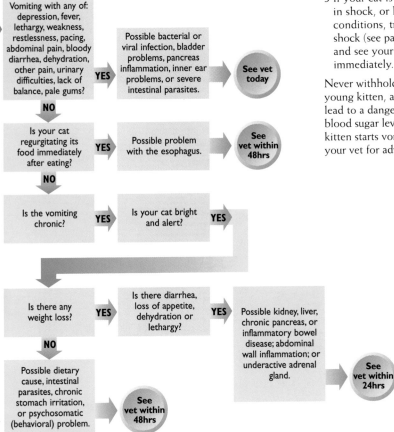

DIARRHEA

Diarrhea is most commonly caused by parasites or the wrong diet. It may, however, also be associated with infections, malabsorption problems, tumors, allergies, or metabolic disorders. It is the way the body rids itself quickly of substances that causes irritation. In that sense, acute diarrhea is an effective form of defense. Chronic diarrhea always warrants a trip to the vet.

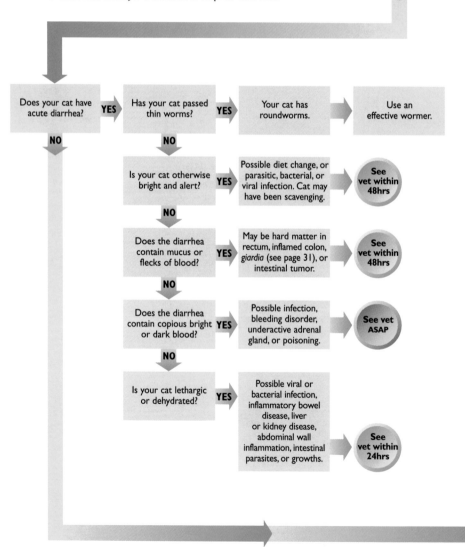

Current symptoms

Does your cat have acute diarrhea? **YES** → Has your cat passed thin worms? **YES** → Your cat has roundworms. → Use an effective wormer.

NO ↓ **NO** ↓

Is your cat otherwise bright and alert? **YES** → Possible diet change, or parasitic, bacterial, or viral infection. Cat may have been scavenging. → **See vet within 48hrs**

NO ↓

Does the diarrhea contain mucus or flecks of blood? **YES** → May be hard matter in rectum, inflamed colon, *giardia* (see page 31), or intestinal tumor. → **See vet within 48hrs**

NO ↓

Does the diarrhea contain copious bright or dark blood? **YES** → Possible infection, bleeding disorder, underactive adrenal gland, or poisoning. → **See vet ASAP**

NO ↓

Is your cat lethargic or dehydrated? **YES** → Possible viral or bacterial infection, inflammatory bowel disease, liver or kidney disease, abdominal wall inflammation, intestinal parasites, or growths. → **See vet within 24hrs**

HOME TREATMENT FOR DIARRHEA

Most episodes of diarrhea soon correct themselves. The affected cat quickly and efficiently gets rid of what is irritating its bowels.

After an episode of diarrhea, feed your cat a meal that is easy to digest–for example, fat-free chicken and rice. Foods with a good balance of soluble and insoluble fiber enhance the return of good microbes and suppress the growth of unwanted ones. Many commercially produced foods are beneficial for fiber balance.

DEHYDRATION

A loss of body fluid is associated with vomiting and diarrhea. Losses also occur when a cat has a fever, heat prostration, or no water to drink.

Dehydration can be serious. Normally, if you pinch the skin on your cat's neck, it snaps back into place immediately. Dehydration causes a loss of skin elasticity. If the skin does not retract instantly, as it normally does, your cat is probably dehydrated (see page 20). Contact your veterinarian immediately.

If your cat has an increased appetite but is losing weight, see your vet.

Does your cat have chronic diarrhea, but no other clinical signs? **YES** → Possible dietary allergy or intolerance to diet, inflammatory bowel disease, or parasites. → **See vet within 48hrs**

NO ↓

Is your cat suffering from chronic diarrhea and weight loss? **YES** → Does your cat have loss of appetite? **YES** → May be kidney, liver, or endocrine disorders, parasites, infectious diseases, or tumors. → **See vet within 48hrs**

NO ↓   **NO** ↓

Does your cat have an increased appetite? **YES** → Possible bowel disease or problem with the intestines, pancreas, or thyroid. → **See vet within 48hrs**

NO ↓

Possible parasites, or inflammatory bowel disease. → **See vet within 24hrs**

Does your cat have diarrhea with black, tarry stools? **YES** → Possible stomach conditions involving bleeding. → **See vet within 24hrs**

BOWEL PROBLEMS

Mild constipation, lasting a day, is of no clinical importance and is usually caused by a cat eating something indigestible, often too much bone. Constipation lasting more than a day, or straining as a consequence of diarrhea, warrants professional advice or intervention. It is surprisingly simple to confuse straining to urinate with straining to defecate. If unsure, see your veterinarian the same day.

Current symptoms

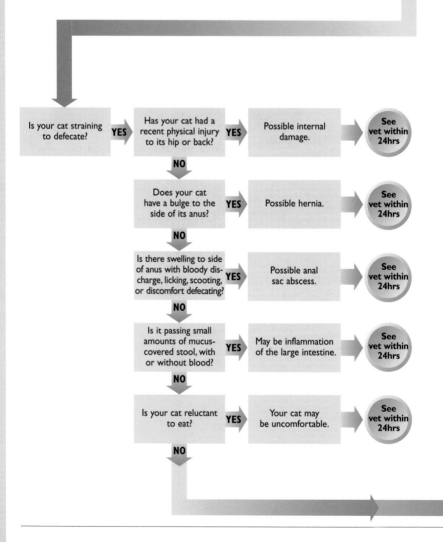

Is your cat straining to defecate? **YES** → Has your cat had a recent physical injury to its hip or back? **YES** → Possible internal damage. → **See vet within 24hrs**

NO ↓

Does your cat have a bulge to the side of its anus? **YES** → Possible hernia. → **See vet within 24hrs**

NO ↓

Is there swelling to side of anus with bloody discharge, licking, scooting, or discomfort defecating? **YES** → Possible anal sac abscess. → **See vet within 24hrs**

NO ↓

Is it passing small amounts of mucus-covered stool, with or without blood? **YES** → May be inflammation of the large intestine. → **See vet within 24hrs**

NO ↓

Is your cat reluctant to eat? **YES** → Your cat may be uncomfortable. → **See vet within 24hrs**

NO ↓

TREATING CONSTIPATION

If your cat's stools are small and hard but your cat is otherwise healthy, add fiber to its diet or give it a cat laxative. This is usually a pleasant-tasting food mixture with liquid paraffin added. If your cat has not defecated for more than two days or is uncomfortable, see your veterinarian, who may give it an enema. Do not use over-the-counter enemas or laxatives made for humans. Some of these can be irritating, and even dangerous, to cats.

CONSTIPATION, DIARRHEA, OR URINARY TRACT DISEASE?

Straining can be associated with inflammation of the bowels, hard stools in the large intestine, or a urinary problem. Always check on what has preceded an episode of straining to ensure correct diagnosis. If your cat has just had diarrhea, it is likely to be straining because of inflamed bowels caused by the diarrhea. Straining is more likely to be associated with lower urinary tract disease than with a bowel disorder.

If your cat is clearly spending longer than usual at the litter tray and seems to be in discomfort, examine the stools to see whether constipation is the problem.

FEEDING BONES

Eating bones is an excellent way for a cat to massage its teeth and gums. Too many bones, however, will cause constipation, particularly in older cats. One cooked chicken neck a week is usually fine, but must be given under your constant supervision to ensure the bones are not swallowed.

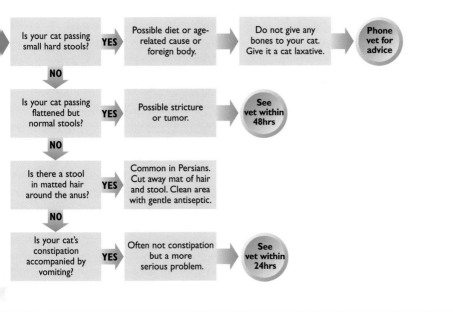

Is your cat passing small hard stools? → **YES** → Possible diet or age-related cause or foreign body. → Do not give any bones to your cat. Give it a cat laxative. → **Phone vet for advice**

NO ↓

Is your cat passing flattened but normal stools? → **YES** → Possible stricture or tumor. → **See vet within 48hrs**

NO ↓

Is there a stool in matted hair around the anus? → **YES** → Common in Persians. Cut away mat of hair and stool. Clean area with gentle antiseptic.

NO ↓

Is your cat's constipation accompanied by vomiting? → **YES** → Often not constipation but a more serious problem. → **See vet within 24hrs**

DISTENDED ABDOMEN

The only normal cause of a distended abdomen is pregnancy–all others are abnormal. A potbelly may be due to being overweight. A distended abdomen may occur if gas accumulates in the intestines, or it may be a sign of worms. More worrying, a distended abdomen may be caused by fluid in the abdominal cavity, obstruction to the urinary tract, enlargement of the liver or spleen, or abdominal tumors.

Current symptoms

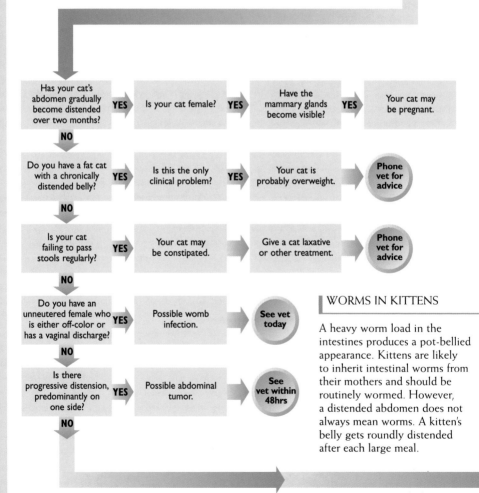

Has your cat's abdomen gradually become distended over two months? **YES** → Is your cat female? **YES** → Have the mammary glands become visible? **YES** → Your cat may be pregnant.

NO ↓

Do you have a fat cat with a chronically distended belly? **YES** → Is this the only clinical problem? **YES** → Your cat is probably overweight. → **Phone vet for advice**

NO ↓

Is your cat failing to pass stools regularly? **YES** → Your cat may be constipated. → Give a cat laxative or other treatment. → **Phone vet for advice**

NO ↓

Do you have an unneutered female who is either off-color or has a vaginal discharge? **YES** → Possible womb infection. → **See vet today**

NO ↓

Is there progressive distension, predominantly on one side? **YES** → Possible abdominal tumor. → **See vet within 48hrs**

NO ↓

WORMS IN KITTENS

A heavy worm load in the intestines produces a pot-bellied appearance. Kittens are likely to inherit intestinal worms from their mothers and should be routinely wormed. However, a distended abdomen does not always mean worms. A kitten's belly gets roundly distended after each large meal.

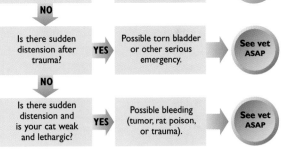

Is there progressive round distension?	**YES** → Possible heart or liver disease, FIP, cancer, or peritonitis (inflamed abdominal lining).	→ **See vet within 24hrs**
NO ↓		
Is there sudden distension after trauma?	**YES** → Possible torn bladder or other serious emergency.	→ **See vet ASAP**
NO ↓		
Is there sudden distension and is your cat weak and lethargic?	**YES** → Possible bleeding (tumor, rat poison, or trauma).	→ **See vet ASAP**

ABDOMINAL FAT FLAPS

A cat naturally stores excess fat in its belly and in the tissue between the abdomen and the skin. This fat deposit in the region of the mammary glands can become dramatically large. It may be pendulous, even flap from side to side when a cat runs. It occurs more commonly in neutered cats, especially in long, lean breeds such as the Siamese. It is an aesthetic rather than a veterinary problem.

HEART DISEASE

Heart disease is more common in cats than was once realized. In some cats, the inefficiency of the heart causes blood to back up, which causes swelling to the liver. Eventually, fluid weeps from the surface of the liver and accumulates in the abdominal cavity, causing pot-bellied distension.

FELINE INFECTIOUS PERITONITIS (FIP)

Feline infectious peritonitis (FIP) is a genetic mutation of a feline coronavirus (FeCV).

An accumulation of fluid in the abdominal cavity, producing a pot-bellied appearance, is a classic sign of FIP, especially in young cats. It may, however, also produce a variety of lesser symptoms (see page 25).

There is a blood test available for FeCV in general, but not one specifically for FIP. A positive FeCV blood test does not confirm that a cat has FIP, only that it has a feline coronavirus.

A diagnosis of FIP is based upon clinical signs, together with a positive FeCV blood test.

Neutered cats may develop a pendulous abdominal flap. However, this is not a veterinary problem.

EXCESSIVE DRINKING

Excessive drinking can be the first outward sign of an internal problem. It can also be associated with excessive urinating. If you think your cat's drinking has increased, organize a visit to your veterinarian, especially if your cat is over eight years old, very overweight, or prone to sugar diabetes. Whenever possible, take a urine sample to your veterinarian.

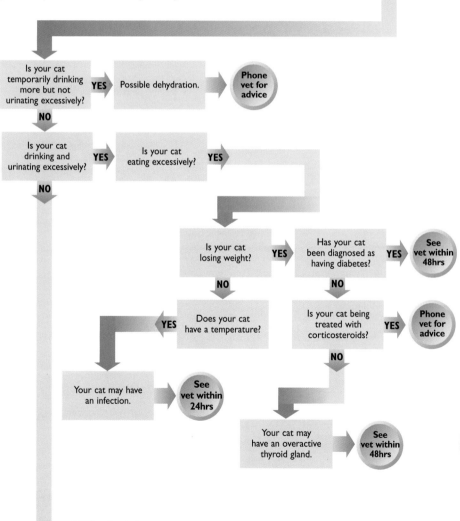

DRINKING AND OLDER CATS

All cats drink more if their diet changes from wet to dry food, if they are hot, after physical exercise, and even after mental activity.

However, excessive drinking is always of clinical significance. Your older cat should not drink more than it did when it was younger.

If you think your cat is drinking more, provide measured quantities for a few days and record how much the cat drinks. Take this information and a sample of your cat's morning urine, stored in a clean jar, to your veterinarian.

If your cat is drinking more than usual, take it to see your veterinarian. Excessive drinking may be an indication of serious illness.

SUGAR DIABETES AND YOUR CAT

Diabetes is a condition in which there is excess sugar in the blood. Insulin, produced in the pancreas, controls blood sugar.

If a cat fails to produce sufficient insulin, it may be necessary to give insulin by injection to control the life-threatening consequences of diabetes.

Fortunately, in some cats, diabetes can be controlled with high-fiber diets. In others, the condition is temporary, spontaneously resolving after a period of insulin treatment.

LITTER TRAY WATCHING

It may be difficult to observe whether your cat is drinking more, especially if there are several sources of water. If your cat uses a litter tray and it appears to need changing more frequently, this is an excellent clue that your cat is drinking more.

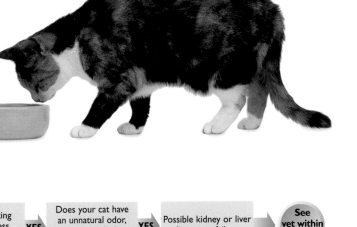

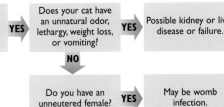

Is your cat eating normally or less than usual? **YES** → Does your cat have an unnatural odor, lethargy, weight loss, or vomiting? **YES** → Possible kidney or liver disease or failure. → **See vet within 24hrs**

NO ↓

Do you have an unneutered female? **YES** → May be womb infection. → **See vet ASAP**

URINARY PROBLEMS

Straining to urinate is not uncommon, especially in overweight, indoor, sedentary male cats. It may, however, be a sign of a life-threatening condition–a blockage of the urinary tract. If you have an outdoor male cat, watch for signs of bladder blockage; see if he licks his prepuce frequently, appears in pain, loses his appetite, or vomits. Excess urinating is always significant and warrants a visit to the veterinarian.

Current symptoms

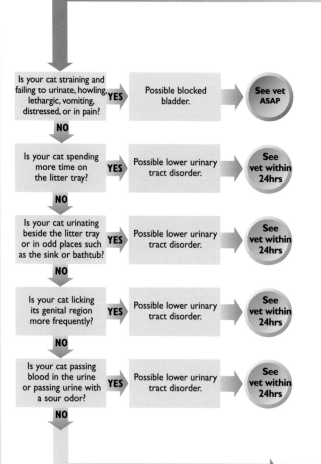

Is your cat straining and failing to urinate, howling, lethargic, vomiting, distressed, or in pain? **YES** → Possible blocked bladder. → **See vet ASAP**

NO

Is your cat spending more time on the litter tray? **YES** → Possible lower urinary tract disorder. → **See vet within 24hrs**

NO

Is your cat urinating beside the litter tray or in odd places such as the sink or bathtub? **YES** → Possible lower urinary tract disorder. → **See vet within 24hrs**

NO

Is your cat licking its genital region more frequently? **YES** → Possible lower urinary tract disorder. → **See vet within 24hrs**

NO

Is your cat passing blood in the urine or passing urine with a sour odor? **YES** → Possible lower urinary tract disorder. → **See vet within 24hrs**

NO

LOWER URINARY TRACT DISORDERS

A cat straining to urinate may have a lower urinary tract problem. Vets have a variety of names for this condition. Once called feline urologic syndrome (FUS), it is now called feline lower urinary tract disease (FLUTD). The name has changed because, although veterinarians know it is rarely caused by infection, they are still uncertain about the exact causes of this problem. Some cats show few clinical signs before they become seriously ill with a life-threatening urinary blockage.

Always contact your veterinarian for advice if you see your cat straining to urinate.

URINE COLOR

The color of your cat's urine is a clue to its health. Dark or orange-colored urine means that it is concentrated and may indicate that your cat has a liver or an immune condition. Concentrated urine may also be due to retention or dehydration. Light to colorless urine indicates dilute urine, and is often associated with diabetes or kidney disease.

MALES AND FEMALES

The female cat's urinary tract anatomy increases her risk of feline lower urinary tract disease (FLUTD). However, the vast majority of urinary obstructions occur in male cats. The male lower urinary tract, the urethra, is very narrow, and sediment, mucus, or bladder stones can block it, causing a painful and life-threatening obstruction.

OUTDOOR CATS

Changes in urinating behavior are more difficult to observe in cats that toilet outdoors. However, individuals with urinary disorders may spend more time indoors and lick their genitals more frequently.

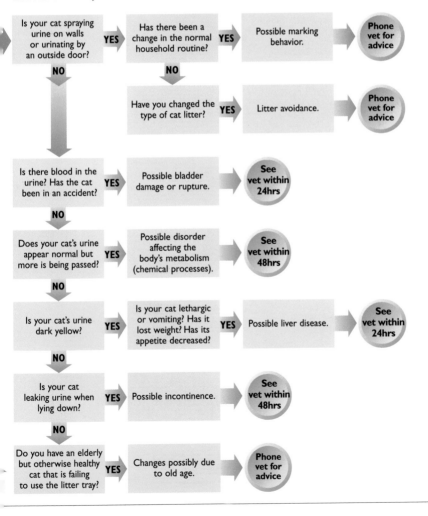

GENITAL DISCHARGES

Genital discharges are always significant. In females, a green, yellow, or cream-colored discharge may indicate a mild to life-threatening womb infection. Both females and males may produce genital discharges associated with feline lower urinary tract disease (FLUTD). These discharges resemble plain or gritty mucus and are usually accompanied by straining to urinate.

Female: current symptoms   **Male: current symptoms**

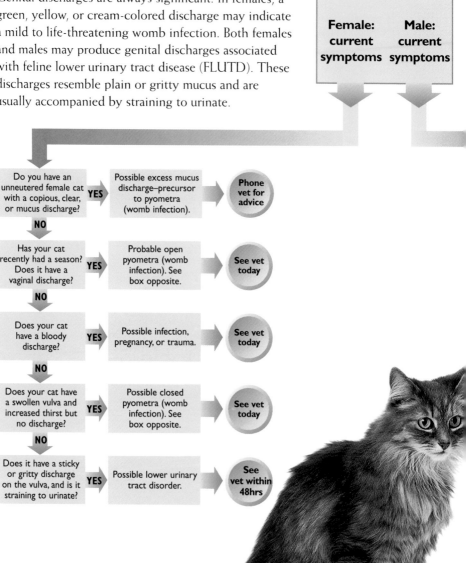

Do you have an unneutered female cat with a copious, clear, or mucus discharge? **YES** → Possible excess mucus discharge—precursor to pyometra (womb infection). → **Phone vet for advice**

NO ↓

Has your cat recently had a season? Does it have a vaginal discharge? **YES** → Probable open pyometra (womb infection). See box opposite. → **See vet today**

NO ↓

Does your cat have a bloody discharge? **YES** → Possible infection, pregnancy, or trauma. → **See vet today**

NO ↓

Does your cat have a swollen vulva and increased thirst but no discharge? **YES** → Possible closed pyometra (womb infection). See box opposite. → **See vet today**

NO ↓

Does it have a sticky or gritty discharge on the vulva, and is it straining to urinate? **YES** → Possible lower urinary tract disorder. → **See vet within 48hrs**

A female cat may suffer from a womb infection. If left untreated, this may be life-threatening for your cat.

PYOMETRA (WOMB INFECTION)

Older, unneutered females, especially those that have never produced kittens, have an ever-increasing risk of womb infection following a season. Bacteria gain access to the womb during estrus.

An individual with an open pyometra has a repellent and obvious vaginal discharge.

If the cervix closes down after infection gains entry, a closed pyometra develops. This is more toxic, more dangerous, and more difficult to diagnose. If your female cat has recently been in season and is now behaving uncharacteristically, see your veterinarian immediately.

GENITAL OR URINARY DISCHARGE

Irritation to the urinary system may stimulate the production of protective mucus, which is then discharged. It can be difficult to determine whether this mucus is coming from the urinary or reproductive tracts. Similarly, blood may come from the reproductive or urinary tracts.

Your veterinarian will examine the discharge and treat the appropriate system.

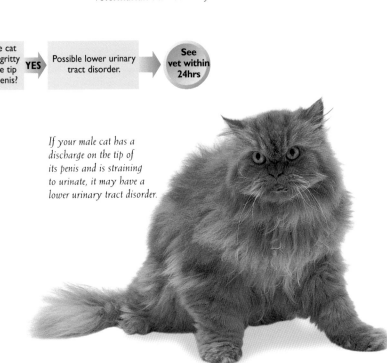

Does your male cat have a sticky or gritty discharge on the tip of prepuce or penis? **YES** Possible lower urinary tract disorder. **See vet within 24hrs**

If your male cat has a discharge on the tip of its penis and is straining to urinate, it may have a lower urinary tract disorder.

LABOR AND BIRTH

If you know your cat is pregnant, plan ahead.
Contact your vet to ensure guidance is available when
it is needed most. Small litters of large kittens passing
through a narrow birth canal may cause difficulties,
as may weak contractions. Older, overweight,
and nervous cats are more likely to have weaker
contractions. Very young cats may need a little help
cleaning their kittens to stimulate breathing.

**Current
symptoms**

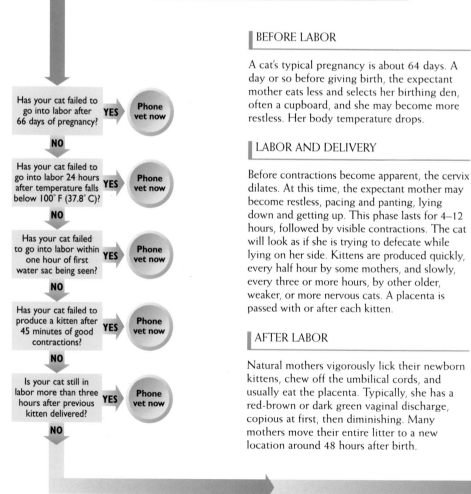

Has your cat failed to go into labor after 66 days of pregnancy? **YES** → **Phone vet now**

NO

Has your cat failed to go into labor 24 hours after temperature falls below 100° F (37.8° C)? **YES** → **Phone vet now**

NO

Has your cat failed to go into labor within one hour of first water sac being seen? **YES** → **Phone vet now**

NO

Has your cat failed to produce a kitten after 45 minutes of good contractions? **YES** → **Phone vet now**

NO

Is your cat still in labor more than three hours after previous kitten delivered? **YES** → **Phone vet now**

NO

BEFORE LABOR

A cat's typical pregnancy is about 64 days. A
day or so before giving birth, the expectant
mother eats less and selects her birthing den,
often a cupboard, and she may become more
restless. Her body temperature drops.

LABOR AND DELIVERY

Before contractions become apparent, the cervix
dilates. At this time, the expectant mother may
become restless, pacing and panting, lying
down and getting up. This phase lasts for 4–12
hours, followed by visible contractions. The cat
will look as if she is trying to defecate while
lying on her side. Kittens are produced quickly,
every half hour by some mothers, and slowly,
every three or more hours, by other older,
weaker, or more nervous cats. A placenta is
passed with or after each kitten.

AFTER LABOR

Natural mothers vigorously lick their newborn
kittens, chew off the umbilical cords, and
usually eat the placenta. Typically, she has a
red-brown or dark green vaginal discharge,
copious at first, then diminishing. Many
mothers move their entire litter to a new
location around 48 hours after birth.

PEACE AND QUIET

Some nervous or worried individuals will stop their labor if they are disturbed. To avoid this:

- Keep visitors away
- Keep all sights and sounds minimal

Has heavy, fresh blood been passed during labor? **YES** → **See vet ASAP**

NO ↓

Has foul smelling, brown or yellow discharge been passed during labor? **YES** → **Phone vet today**

NO ↓

Is the mother weak or listless? **YES** → **See vet ASAP**

NO ↓

Continue with home delivery. → Has bright blood been passed after the delivery finished? **YES** → **Phone vet today**

NO ↓

Was there pus or smelly discharge from vulva after the delivery finished? **YES** → **Phone vet today**

NO ↓

Was the mother panting with increasing intensity after birth? **YES** → **Phone vet today**

NO ↓

Do the mother or kittens look weak, sick, or depressed? **YES** → **Phone vet today**

NO ↓

Continue with home care.

The mother cat should look bright and content and the kittens should be alert and feeding well.

SURPRISING PREGNANCY

Cats are superbly efficient during pregnancy. Some of them gain little weight and, retain their figures until just before giving birth.

It is not unusual for an outdoor cat to take up residence in a new home a few weeks before giving birth. If you have taken on a stray cat, always be prepared for the possibility of an extra furry surprise.

GLOSSARY

Abscess A localized pocket of infection that forms a very painful swelling.

Acute Condition occurs suddenly, as in acute pain.

Adjuvant A substance that aids another. Enhances the power of vaccines.

Adrenal gland Gland beside each kidney responsible for producing a variety of hormones.

Allergy An increased reactivity of immune system cells to anything in the environment.

Anaphylactic shock An exaggerated and potentially life-threatening over-reaction of the immune system.

Anemia Reduced red blood cells, related to cancers, blood loss, bone marrow suppression, parasites, or immune-mediated disease that destroys red blood cells.

Antihistamine A drug that counteracts the effects of histamine.

Arthritis Inflammation of a joint.

Asthma A condition involving spasm of the muscles in the air passages resulting in difficulty breathing.

Benign A local tumor that does not spread, that is to say, it is not malignant.

Biopsy The collection of tissue for microscopic examination.

Bronchitis Inflammation of air passages.

Carcinoma A malignant tumor originating in skin cells or cells that line the internal organs.

Cardiovascular Pertaining to the heart and circulation.

Cataract Crystalline cloudiness to the lens of the eye.

Cheyletiella mites A contagious external parasite primarily affecting young dogs and cats. It can also temporarily affect people.

Chlamydia A family of bacteria with some of the characteristics of viruses.

Chronic A condition that has existed for some time.

Clinical signs What you observe your cat doing.

Colitis Inflamed large intestine.

Congenital A condition present at birth that may or may not be hereditary.

Conjunctivitis Inflammation of the membranes of the eyes and eyelids.

Cornea The clear surface of the eyeball.

Corticosteroid Any of the hormones produced by the adrenal cortex.

Cyanotic shock Shock associated with a lack of oxygen-carrying hemoglobin in the blood.

Cyst A sac filled with glandular secretion.

Dehydration Loss of natural level of liquid in body tissue.

Dermatitis Inflammation of the skin.

Diabetes insipidus Deficiency in pituitary hormone (antidiuretic hormone or ADH) that controls urine concentration in the kidneys. Causes excessive drinking and urinating.

Diabetes mellitus or sugar diabetes
High blood sugar, either because of a lack
of insulin production or because body
tissue cannot absorb
circulating insulin.
Diaphragm Thin
involuntary muscle that
separates the chest cavity from
the abdomen.
Drooling Dribbling.
Ear mites Tiny parasites that
live in the ear canal and
cause irritation.
Eclampsia A seizure-like condition
affecting nursing mothers, caused by low
calcium levels in the blood.
Eczema A general term describing any
type of superficial skin inflammation.
Edema Excessive accumulation
of fluid in body tissue.
Endocrine Pertaining to the major
hormonal systems of the body, including
the pituitary, adrenal, thyroid, and
sex hormones.
Enema A solution introduced into
the rectum.
Enteritis Inflammation of the intestines.
Enzyme deficiency A deficiency of
digestive enzymes.
Eosinophilic granuloma Nodules
on the skin, lips, or gums containing
accumulations of white blood cells
called eosinophils.
Eosinophilic plaque Well-defined, often
ulcerated, itchy lesions. They most
frequently occur on the back, hind legs,
and groin, and contain accumulations
of eosinophils.
Epilepsy Temporary disturbance to the
nervous system caused by excessive
electrical activity in the brain.
Esophagus The connection between
the pharynx and the stomach.

Estrus The period in the
reproductive cycle during
which eggs are produced
and released.
Feline coronavirus
A nonpathogenic
virus commonly found in
cats. This virus can mutate
into a pathogenic strain,
causing feline infectious
peritonitis or FIP.
FeLV Feline Leukemia Virus,
a potentially lethal virus
that can be transmitted by a
mother cat to her young and
also through saliva.
Fenbendazole Wormer, with the trade-
name Panacur.
FIP Feline Infectious Peritonitis, the
disease mutation of Feline coronavirus.
Fipronyl Topical flea killer, with the
trade-name Frontline.
FIV Feline Immunodeficiency Virus, a
virus associated with a variety of serious,
potentially lethal, diseases.
Fleas The most common external
parasite living on a cat's skin. Fleas live
by feeding on blood. Cats may sometimes
be sensitive to bites or flea dirt.
Gastrointestinal Pertaining to the
stomach and intestines.
Geriatrics An area of medicine dealing
with the problems and illnesses associated
with aging and the elderly.
Giardia A protozoal intestinal parasite
capable of causing diarrhea.
Gingivitis Inflammation to the gums at
edge of teeth, caused by tartar buildup.
Glaucoma Increased fluid pressure
inside the eye.
Granuloma A benign connective
tissue mass associated with irritation
or inflammation.

Heartworms Parasites living in the heart. Larvae are transmitted by mosquitoes. More common in dogs than in cats.

Hematoma A blood-filled swelling.

Hemorrhage Bleeding.

Hereditary An inherited condition, that is passed on in the genes.

Hernia The protrusion of a body part out of the cavity in which it is normally located.

Hookworms Blood-sucking worms that live in the small intestine.

Imidocloprid Topical flea killer, with the trade-name Advantage.

Immune-mediated disease A condition caused by an overreaction of the immune system.

Incontinence Uncontrolled dribbling of urine, especially when lying down. More common in older and neutered female cats.

Inflammatory bowel disease Any bowel disease that is associated with inflammation.

-itis An inflammation.

Laryngitis Inflammation to the opening of the windpipe.

Laxative A medicine that loosens bowel contents and helps evacuation.

Lesion A change to body tissue caused by disease or trauma.

Lice Parasites that suck blood, causing anemia in a severe infestation.

Lufenuron An insect development inhibitor used for flea control.

Lungworms A rare worm in cats, technically called *aelurostrongylus abstrusus*.

Lymphoma A tumor arising from lymph tissue.

Malabsorption A condition in which nutrients are poorly absorbed into the circulation from the small intestines.

Malignant A tumor that has the potential to spread (metastasize) to other parts of the body.

Mastitis Inflammation of mammary tissue.

Metabolic disorder An abnormality of any of the body's metabolic functions.

Metastasize Spread to other parts of the body.

Mucometra A womb that is filled with mucus.

Mucus Clear, lubricating secretion produced by cells in mucous membranes.

Myositis Inflammation of muscle.

Noradrenalin A neurohormone that constricts blood vessels and increases the heart rate and blood pressure.

Nystagmus A rhythmic and involuntary movement of both eyes in unison.

Ophthalmologist A specialist in diseases and conditions of the eyes.

-osis A disease condition. For example, nephrosis is a disease condition of the kidneys. Nephritis is specifically an inflammation to the kidneys.

Parvovirus A virus that causes severe damage to the lining of the intestines and may also suppress the immune system. Commonly called feline enteritis or feline panleukopenia.

Pathology The study of damaging changes to tissue.

Perianal Around the anus, as in perianal adenomas.

Perineal The regions on either side of the anus, as in perineal hernia.

Peritonitis Inflammation of the lining of the abdominal cavity.

Pneumonia Inflammation of lung tissue.

Poly- Excessive or multiple, as in polyarthritis.

Praziquantel Wormer, with the trade-name Drontal Plus.

Pulmonary Relating to the lungs.

Pus A mixture of bacteria and dead white blood cells, usually malodorous.

Pyo- Pus related, as in pyometra, a pus-filled womb.

Pyometra A pus-filled womb.

Rabies Fatal viral disease affecting nervous system. Usually transmitted through a bite from an affected animal.

Regurgitation Expelling food from the esophagus.

Retina The light-sensitive layers of cells at the back of the eyes.

Ringworm A fungal infection of the skin that causes scaly skin and irritation. Ringworm is not caused by worms.

Roundworms Parasites that live in a cat's digestive tract, feeding on digested food.

Sarcoma A malignant tumor formed from body-tissue cells.

Sarcoptic mange An extremely itchy, crusty skin condition caused by *sarcoptes scabiei*, a burrowing external parasite.

Scabies Another name for sarcoptic mange.

Sclerosis Hardening of tissue, as a consequence of age or inflammation.

Scooting Dragging the bottom on the ground. Caused by anal irritation.

Selamectin Topical flea repellent, with the trade-name Revolution.

Shock A medical emergency in which the cardiovascular system collapses, causing physical collapse, rapid pulse, and pale mucous membranes.

Sinusitis Inflammation to the sinuses.

Spay To surgically remove ovaries and uterus to prevent estrus and pregnancy.

Stricture Narrowing of a tube or passage.

Tapeworms Intestinal parasites that feed on a cat's partially digested food.

Thyroid gland The glands in the neck responsible for producing hormones that control the body's metabolism.

Thyroid problem Commonly an overactive thyroid gland. Rarely an underactive thyroid gland.

Toxoplasmosis Diseases caused by parasite, often in raw meat, which affects digestive system. Can sometimes be transmitted to humans.

Trauma Injury or damage caused by external force.

Tumor A growth of tissue in which cell multiplication is uncontrolled and progressive. Can be benign (local) or malignant (having the ability to spread elsewhere).

Ulcerated Where surface tissue has been lost through damage or disease.

Vestibular Pertaining to the organ of balance in the middle ear, as in vestibular syndrome.

INDEX

A

abdomen 80–1
age 12, 83
aggression 40, 41
Airway–Breathing–
    Circulation check 35
allergic reactions 32, 33
    choking 67
    ears 53
    eyes 50, 51
    licking 47
    nasal disorders 64, 65
anaphylactic shock 32,
    33
appetite 72–3, 77
arthritis 58, 59
artificial respiration 34–5,
    36–7
artificial tears 51
asthma 66

B

balance 60–1
behavior 40–5
    age 12
    indoor problems 11
benign tumors 57
birth 88–9
bites 47
    ears 52, 53
bleeding 48–9
blue-gray eyes 51
body temperature 32
bone chewing 79
bowels 78–9
breast cancer 57
breath 68–9
breathing 25, 70–1
    resuscitation 34–5, 75
    shock 32

C

cancer see feline leukemia
    virus; tumors

capillary refill time
    21, 32
    resuscitation 36
cardiopulmonary
    resuscitation 34–7
cat flu 23, 64
cat scratch disease 14
cataracts 51
cheyletiella mites 55
choking 66–7, 70
claws 59
closed wounds 26
cold compresses 47, 59
comas 63
communication 17
conjunctiva 20, 65
consciousness 34–6, 62
constipation 78–9, 80
contractions 88
convulsions 62–3
coordination 60–1
coughing 66
cryptococcus 65

D

deafness 53
dehydration 20
    diarrhea 77
    drinking 82
    vomiting 75
depression 43
dermatitis 55
diabetes 72, 82–3
diarrhea 76–7, 79
    giardia 30, 31
discharges, genital 86–9
dribbling 69
drinking 82–3
drooling 47

E

ear drops 19
ears 52–3, 54
    mites 28–9, 31

eating 72–3
eclampsia 62
eczema 55
epilepsy 62
examinations 14–21
external parasites 28–9
eye drops 19
eyes 50–1

F

fainting 36
fat flaps 81
feces 78–9
feline chlamydia 23
feline immunodeficiency
    virus 23, 24
feline infectious enteritis
    23, 24
feline infectious peritonitis
    25, 81
    vaccination 23
feline leukemia virus 23,
    24
feline lower urinary tract
    disease 84, 86
feline urologic syndrome
    84
females 13
    discharges 86, 87
    labor 88–9
    urinary problems 85
fights 50, 52
fleas 28–9, 31
    cat scratch disease
    14,
    scratching 54
fungal infections 28, 29

G

gagging 66–7
genital discharges
    86–9
giardia 30–1, 76
glaucoma 51

gums 20–1, 32
  heart failure 36

H
hair 46, 54–5
hairballs 66, 74
halitosis 68–9
handling 14–15
head-to-paw examination
  16–17
heart disease 81
heart failure 36
heart massage 34, 36–7
heart rate 32–3
heartworms 31
heatstroke 71
hypersensitivity 55

IJK
indoor cats 11
infectious diseases 24–5
ingrown nails 58
inherited conditions 11
injuries 46–7
insect bites 47, 53
insulin 63, 83
internal parasites 30–1

L
labor 88–9
lameness 58–9
laryngitis 45
lethargy 42–3
lice 29
licking 47, 74
limping 58–9
lips 21, 54
liquid medicine 19
liver disease 43
lower urinary tract 84,
  86–7
lumps 56–7
lungworms 66

M
males 13
  discharges 86–7
  urinary problems 84,
    85
medicines 18–19, 73
mites 28–9
  ears 53, 54
  skin 54, 55
myositis 59

N
nails 44–5, 58
nasal disorders 64–5
nausea 74, 75
nervous system 63
neutering 13
nose bleeds 64, 65

O
obesity 37
open wounds 27
oral hygiene 68–9
outdoors cats 10–11, 85
  weight 73
overgrown claws 59

PQ
pain perception 11, 42
painkillers 59
panting 45, 71
parasites 28–31, 54
perineal tumors 57
pneumonia 66
poisoning 61, 69
pot bellies 81
pregnancy 88–9
prepuce 84, 87
pressure points 49
pulse rate 32–3
puncture wounds 46
purring 45
pyometra 86, 87

R
rabies 25
  vaccinations 23,
    40
restlessness 45, 75
restraint 18
resuscitation 34–7
ringworm 28–9, 55
roundworms 30, 31
  diarrhea 76
  vomiting 74
routines 43, 45
  eating 72

S
saliva cysts 69
sarcomas 22
scabies 31, 54
  humans 29
sclerosis 51
scratching
  ears 52
  parasites 28, 29
  skin 54–5
seizures 62–3
septic shock 32
sex 13, 85–7
shock 32–3
  bleeding 48–9
  breathing 70–1
sinusitis 65
skin 20
  allergies 32, 53
  lumps 56–7
  parasites 28
  scratching 54–5
  wounds 26–7
sleeping 45
snake bites 47
sneezing 64, 66
solar dermatitis 55
sound 44–5
stools 78–9
strokes 61

swellings 54, 56–7
symptoms charts
    38–89

T
tablets 18
tapeworms 30, 31
tears, artificial 51
teeth 68
ticks 28, 29
tourniquets 48
toxic painkillers 59
toxoplasmosis 30, 31
trauma 64

tumors 56–7
    abdominal 80
    oral 69
    sarcomas 22
    vaccine-related 22

U
ulcers 69
unconsciousness 34–6, 62
    choking 67
upper respiratory tract
    infections 25
urinary problems 79,
    84–7

V
vaccinations 22–3
    rabies 40
vacuuming 29
vaginal discharges 86–9
vomiting 74–5

WXYZ
weight 16, 80
    outdoors cats 73
wheezing 71
whipworms 30, 31
worms 30–1, 80
wounds 26–7, 46–9.

ACKNOWLEDGMENTS

Produced for Dorling Kindersley Limited by Design Revolution Limited, Queens Park Villa, 30 West Drive, Brighton, East Sussex BN2 0QW

Editorial Director Ian Whitelaw
Senior Designer Lucie Penn
Project Editor Julie Whitaker

Thanks to Chris Lawrence at the RSPCA and my other veterinary colleagues for all their practical suggestions. As ever I'm grateful to my veterinary nurses, Hester Small, Hilary Hayward, Sarah Wilsdon, Amanda Hackett, Ashley McManus, and Jenny Ward for their experience and cheery efficiency running the veterinary clinic.

Publisher's acknowledgments

Dorling Kindersley would like to thank the following:

Photography
All photography by Jane Burton, Angelika Elsebach, Steve Gorton, Marc Henrie, Dave King, Tim Ridley, except:

RSPCA Photolibrary 32; /Angela Hampton 20; 21; 22; 24; /Alan Towse 81. Sally Anne Thompson Animal Photography 10.